BEASTLY BEST BITS

THE EXECUTIONER'S CUT

Terry Deary Illustrated By Martin Brown

IT'S AHEAD OF THE REST!

SCHOLASTIC

www.horrible-histories.co.uk

www.terry-deary.com

Scholastic Children's Books,
Euston House,
24 Eversholt Street,
London NW1 1DB, UK

A division of Scholastic Ltd
London ~ New York ~ Toronto ~ Sydney ~ Auckland
Mexico City ~ New Delhi ~ Hong Kong

Published in the UK by Scholastic Ltd, 2013
Text copyright © Terry Deary, 1993–2013
Illustrations copyright © Martin Brown, 1993–2013

ISBN 978 1407 13610 3

Printed and bound by Tien Wah Press Pte. Ltd, Singapore

2 4 6 8 10 9 7 5 3

Additional artwork:
Copyright © Philip Reeve: from *Rowdy Revolutions* P12–13, 52–53, from *Dark Knights and Dingy Castles* P38–39, from *Incredible Incas* P44–45, from *Wicked Words* P46–47
Copyright © Mike Phillips: from *Dublin* P19, from *Cruel Crime* P20–21, from *Rotten Rulers* P34–35, from *Witches* P50–51, from *Spies* P76–77

Additional colour by:
Rob Davis, Atholl McDonald, Geri Ford

Terrible Team past and present:
Marina Chester, Cat Clarke, Kate Davies, Lisa Edwards, David Fickling, Alison Gadsby, Vicky Garrard, Helen Greathead, Rebecca Lee, Corinne Lucas, Jill Sawyer, Richard Smith, Tracey Turner, Ness Wood

CONTENTS

Dear Reader

In 1993 a series of funny little books slithered onto the bookshelves and into the hearts and minds of readers. These 'History' books turned school-book boredom into gasps and groans, grins and grimaces. They were called Horrible Histories.

They changed the world. Parents discovered their square-eyed, computer-age children suddenly had an interest in 'reading' when they picked up the HH titles. They collected facts like lorries collect hedgehogs and used those facts to pester their parents and torment their teachers with the foulest of those facts ... and a lot of very bad jokes. Teenagers found they wanted to study 'History' at university, and even the terrible teachers turned the pages to find the foul facts that would make their history lessons lively.

Horrible Histories rolled on like a snowball. After five years the books became a magazine collection, museum exhibitions and record-breaking theatre productions. Word got around ... around the world, and soon these funny little books were popular from Australia to Alaska, Serbia to Swansea.

After a dozen years the theatre shows began to tour and bring audiences the horrors of history in 3D. Computer games, board games and web sites all discovered they could join the fun. Along came the Horrible Histories television series that is so popular the production company are beating off awards with a stick - 'adult' comedy awards because adults enjoy the horrors of history too.

Horrible Histories have been around so long they have made history. Now there's a funny thought.

Terry Deary

Dear Reader

How the heck did Horrible Histories get to here?

Now I come to think of it, the first Horrible Histories wasn't even a Horrible Histories, it was a book called The Life and Times of Christobel Colon – a sort of history of Christopher Columbus. It was such fun to illustrate I asked our lovely editor if we could do some more. She looked up from behind her desk and said, "Hold that thought, There's something come in I think you might like". That was the first I heard of Terry Deary and the books that became The Horrible Histories.

Before long we were round a table, thinking about what the covers for these new books should look like. A few scribbles later and The Terrible Tudors executioner and his "Just a little off the top" victim were born. History with the nasty bits left in.

That's how it all began – four people sitting around a table. But as the Horrible Histories grew so did the number of people involved, and today the table of four has become the dining hall of hundreds – computer games people, translator people, TV and theatre people, jigsaw people, more publisher people and many more besides – and every single one deserves my heartfelt thanks.

But … none of them, none of us, is more important than you, faithful and happy fan. Without you Horrible Histories would not have got past the first book. Without your strange taste for tales of torture and hankering for head-hacking humour we wouldn't be here today. Without you Horrible Histories would just be horrible history.

So thank you, each and every one of you. You have made Horrible Histories what it is – you sick and twisted weirdos.

Martin Brown

INTRODUCTION

History is horrible. And school history has never been popular. A bit like me, really. It is so-o-o unfair. Yes. All right. I chop people's heads off from time to time, but I am only doing my job. I'm not cruel. I am just making a bit of money to feed my family. A hairdresser does the same. I just chop a bit more off. Mind you, in history there have been horrible people who have done hideous things to helpless victims. People like Vlad Tepes.

I USED TO TAKE MY PRISONERS OF WAR AND STICK EACH OF THEM ON TOP OF A SHARPENED POLE. THEY SCREAMED AND DIED WHILE I ENJOYED MY DINNER.

See what I mean? Me chopping off your head would be kind compared to that.

Yes, it's true, we sometimes gave a bit of pain. I remember the tale of Mary Queen of Scots execution back in Tudor times.

✹ The axe-man's assistant held her body steady while the axe fell. It missed the neck and cut into the back of her head. Her servants later said they heard her mutter, "Sweet Jesus."

✹ The second chop was a better shot but it still needed a bit of sawing with the axe to finish it off.

✹ Traitors always had their heads held up for the spectators to look at. The executioner would cry out, "May all traitors die this way!" Mary's executioner picked up the head by the hair ... but no one told him Mary was wearing a wig! The head slipped out and bounced over the scaffold. (Her real hair was short and grey.) The executioner was a bit upset and he forgot his lines. The Protestant priest was left to cry out, "Let this be the end to all the Queen's enemies."

The past could be putrid and the pain of the panicking people in peril was petrifying.

Oh, the stories I could tell you! But what's the use of stories if you don't LEARN something from them, eh?

If you DO invent a time machine this book will offer some top Executioner tips on how to stay alive in the past.

AWFUL ANCIENTS

IF YOU FIND YOURSELF IN MESOPOTAMIA THEN THE TOP TIP IS THIS: DO NOT UPSET THE EMPEROR ASHURNASIRPAL ... HIS EXECUTIONERS HAD SOME REALLY NASTY HABITS ...

Muddy Mesopotamia

Around 5000 BC some Stone Age hunters discovered that Mesopotamian mud grew great crops. So those early humans stopped wandering, hunting and gathering wild fruit and nuts. They stayed there and planted crops – hard work, but at least they didn't have to worry about where the next nut was going to come from.

The Mesopotamians started to build their shelters in groups and they formed the first villages. Then the groups grew larger and formed the first cities with the first kings. The people who built the world's first cities made them from mud bricks – muddy Mesopotamia.

They invented the first writing ... and you know what that means? Someone had to teach the writing skills – so they probably had the first teachers and the first schools! Muddy marvellous!

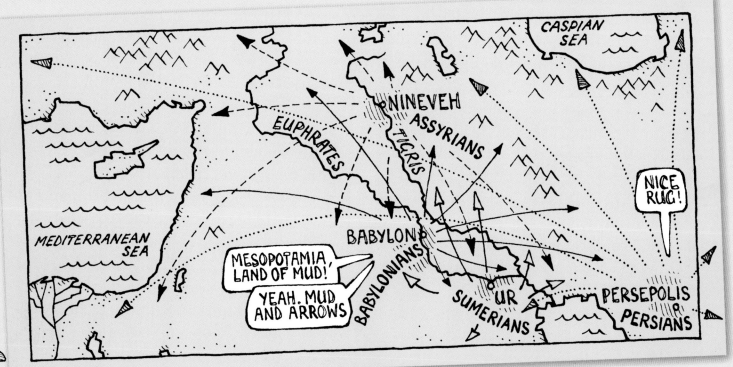

Writing on the wall

Around 2000 BC the Assyrian people fought for their freedom from the Sumerians who ruled Mesopotamia. By 1000 BC they ruled a strong empire with their cruel and ruthless armies.

Ashurnasirpal ruled Assyria around 880 BC and faced many revolutions which he crushed ... cruelly and ruthlessly, of course. In 879 BC he had a 10-day-long party to celebrate the opening of his new palace in Nimrud and he invited 69,574 people.

Generous Ashurnasirpal? Not really. He wanted the guests to see the strength of his defences. The message was: Don't rebel against me.

And they would read on the walls of his palace a description of what he'd done to other rebels. The message was: Or else!

Of course a lot of these old writings get damaged over almost 3,000 years. Can you fit the words back in their right places on this stone tablet?

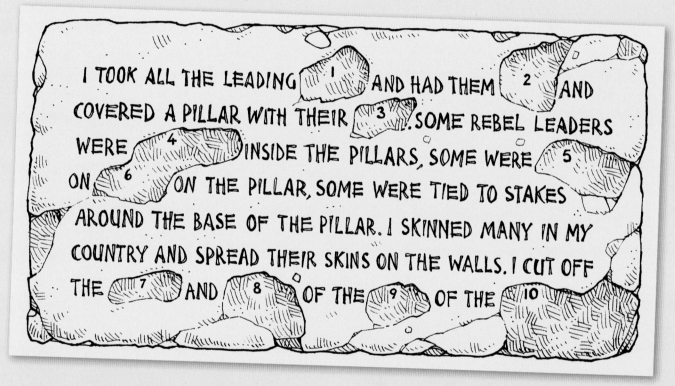

I TOOK ALL THE LEADING ⟨1⟩ AND HAD THEM ⟨2⟩ AND COVERED A PILLAR WITH THEIR ⟨3⟩. SOME REBEL LEADERS WERE ⟨4⟩ INSIDE THE PILLARS, SOME WERE ⟨5⟩ ON ⟨6⟩ ON THE PILLAR, SOME WERE TIED TO STAKES AROUND THE BASE OF THE PILLAR. I SKINNED MANY IN MY COUNTRY AND SPREAD THEIR SKINS ON THE WALLS. I CUT OFF THE ⟨7⟩ AND ⟨8⟩ OF THE ⟨9⟩ OF THE ⟨10⟩

And here are the missing words – but not in the right order!

spikes, revolt, skins, rebels, arms, buried alive, stuck, leaders, legs, skinned

Answers:
1 rebels; 2 skinned; 3 skins; 4 buried alive; 5 stuck; 6 spikes; 7 arms; 8 legs; 9 leaders; 10 revolt. He forgot to add: 'Have a nice nosh!'

Of course even the most ruthless rulers died in time. By 539 BC the Persians had conquered Mesopotamia. The people of the great city of Babylon tried to rebel in 482 BC – but had their mighty walls flattened and their temples destroyed. Bye-bye Mesopotamia, hello Persia!

GRRRR

AWESOME EGYPTIANS

IN EGYPT IT IS BEST NOT TO CRY FOR YOUR MUMMY. YOU MAY JUST GET ONE...

Mad mummies

The ancient Egyptians believed that one day the world would end. When this happened, they thought that everyone who had a body would move on to a wonderful afterlife. But if your body rotted away, you couldn't live in the afterlife. The Egyptians felt it was their duty to make sure that their dead pharaohs didn't rot. So they turned them into mummies.

Could YOU make a mummy? Below is an explanation of how to mummify a body. Unfortunately the instructions have been scrambled by a mummy's curse. Can you rearrange them?

(HORRIBLE HISTORIES NOTE: If you get this completely right then you are an expert mummifier – or 'embalmer' as they were known. You can go out and practise on a favourite dead teacher if you like!)

A. Rip open the front of the body and take out the liver, the stomach, the intestines and the lungs - but leave the heart inside

B. Throw the brain away and pack the skull with 'natron' a sort of salt that stops bodies rotting

C. Stuff the empty body with rags to give it the right shape, then sew it up

D. Take the body to the 'beautiful house' - that's an open-ended tent in the fresh air so the disgusting smell is blown away

E. Wash the liver, the stomach, the intestines and lungs in wine and place them in their own sealed containers - canopic jars

Answers: D, F, J, B, A, E, H, C, I, G

Did you get them right?
Now…
Make a mask that looks like the Pharaoh when he was alive and cover it with gold. Pop him in a stone coffin, stick him in his pyramid and have a party.

Everyone's invited – except the mummy of course.

RUTHLESS ROMANS

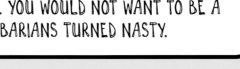

THE ROMAN EMPIRE WAS HUGE. AND NOW IT'S GONE. SERVES THEM RIGHT FOR BEING SO RUTHLESS. YOU WOULD NOT WANT TO BE A ROMAN WHEN THE BARBARIANS TURNED NASTY.

Teutoburger Wald, AD 9

The trouble with General Publius Quintilius Varus was that he was big-headed. You know the sort of person? You can't tell them a *thing*. They think they know it *all*.

Why was such a vain man put in charge of over 10,000 Roman soldiers? Because he was related to the Emperor Augustus, that's why. And Augustus gave Varus a tricky job: to govern the German tribes. But Varus was big-headed, so he thought…

EASY! YOU SEE, THESE GERMAN TRIBES LOVE BEING RULED BY US ROMANS! THEY DO! THEY LOVE US BECAUSE WE ARE SO CIVILIZED!

The truth was that tribes like the Cherusci hated the lousy legions. Of course they *pretended* to be friendly. The son of the Cherusci king,

Arminius, was just waiting for the right moment to strike…

THE ROMANS ARE TO THE SOUTH OF THE TEUTOBURGER FOREST. WE START A LITTLE REBELLION TO THE NORTH. WHEN THE ROMANS MARCH THROUGH THE FOREST WE ATTACK!

And this simple plan worked even though Varus had a warning…

PSST! I'M THE UNCLE OF ARMINIUS. HE PLANS TO AMBUSH YOU IN TEUTOBURGER WALD!

YOU'RE LYING. YOU'RE JUST JEALOUS OF YOUNG ARMINIUS. HE SEEMS LIKE A NICE CHAP FOR A CHERUSCI. WHY, HE'S EVEN OFFERED TO GUIDE US THROUGH THE FOREST!

So the Romans set off to put down the small rebellion. Varus felt so safe he allowed the Romans to take their wives and children on the march. The forest grew thick – but not so thick as Varus – and the paths grew narrow. Arminius and his 'friendly'

Cherusci disappeared into the trees. When they returned they had a huge army of tribesmen.

A thunderstorm turned the tracks into a swamp and the Roman carts were stuck fast. Lightning brought down huge branches and blocked the way. The three Roman legions were trapped. They had to stand there and take the javelins and arrows being shot from the trees. Their shields were soaked and heavy and useless. Varus finally realized his army was going to be wiped out. He wasn't going to let the Germans capture and torture him.

And that's what he did.

But the Roman women and children didn't have swords to fall on. They were captured alive and faced much more grisly deaths. They were sacrificed to the German gods and their intestines were strung from the trees. The next Roman army to arrive was sickened at the sight.

The Romans weren't used to being defeated. Emperor Augustus panicked and lived in fear of the Germans marching into Rome. The worst he got was a grisly present from Arminius … the head of Varus. The big-head had become a dead-head.

Augustus was so upset he refused to cut his hair or shave his beard for months. He wandered around muttering…

While Emperor Augustus moaned this over and over again he often bashed his head against the nearest wall.

As he lay dying, five years after Teutoburger Wald, he muttered…

While Emperor Augustus moaned this over and over again he often bashed his head against the nearest wall.

The Romans clung on to power for another 500 years, but that first defeat at Teutoburger Wald was a terrible shock.

GROOVY GREEKS

IF YOU LIVED IN ANCIENT TIMES YOU SHOULD NOT EVEN THINK ABOUT FEELING POORLY. DOCTORS WERE EVEN MORE DISGUSTING THAN ME WITH MY AXE!

What's up, Doc?

The earliest Greek doctor was said to be called Aesculapius. But, since he was supposed to be the son of a god, he probably didn't exist.

But his followers, the Asculapians, did exist. They didn't work from a hospital, they worked from a temple. Most of their patients recovered with rest, sleep and good food. But Asculapians liked people to think they were gods so the patients had to say prayers and make sacrifices.

The temple was famous because no one ever died in the temple of Aesculapius and his doctor-priests! How did they manage this?

They cheated. If someone was dying when they arrived then they weren't allowed in. And if they started dying once they got inside they were dumped in the nearby woods.

I'M FEELING A LOT BETTER!

The doctor-priests were in it for the money. They warned patients that if they didn't pay, the gods would make them sick again. And they advertised. Carvings in the ruins show the doctor-priests made fantastic claims...

LAST WEEK A ONE-EYED MAN CAME TO THE TEMPLE. WHILE HE SLEPT THE GODS RUBBED OINTMENT ONTO THE EYELID, HE WOKE UP WITH TWO EYES.

SPECIAL OFFER AT THE TEMPLE—TWO FOR THE PRICE OF ONE

A SPARTAN GIRL, ARETE, SUFFERED FROM WATER ON THE BRAIN. AESCULAPIUS SIMPLY CUT OFF HER HEAD AND DRAINED THE WATER OFF. HE THEN CLEVERLY STITCHED THE HEAD BACK ON

BRILLIANT... UNFORTUNATELY HE STITCHED ON THE WRONG HEAD

NERAMUS OF MYTILENE WAS BALD. HIS FRIENDS MADE FUN OF HIM. WHILE HE SLEPT AESCULAPIUS RUBBED OINTMENT IN HIS HEAD. NERAMUS WOKE UP WITH A THICK HEAD OF BLACK HAIR

JUST REMEMBER TO GIVE IT A BOWL OF MILK EVERY DAY—AND KEEP AWAY FROM MICE

Horrible Hippocrates

Hippocrates (460–357 BC) was a Greek doctor who believed in the proper study of the body using experiments.

Hippocrates was so great that today's doctors still take the Oath of Hippocrates (though it has been altered in modern times) and promise:

I will give no deadly medicine to anyone if asked ... I will use treatment to help the sick but never to injure.

Hippo took samples from his patients and tested them. But he couldn't test them in a laboratory with chemicals the way modern doctors can. He tested them by tasting them or by making his patient taste them. But which of the following horrible things were tasted to test? Answer 'Yummy yes' or 'Nasty no'...

1 toenails
2 vomit
3 hair
4 ear wax
5 pus from infected wounds
6 tears
7 skin
8 snot
9 spit
10 pee

Answers:
1 Nasty no; 2 Yummy yes; 3 Nasty no; 4 Yummy yes; 5 Yummy yes; 6 Yummy yes; 7 Nasty no; 8 Yummy yes; 9 Nasty no; 10 Yummy yes.

Next time you feel poorly why not take a bottle of pee and snot along to your doctor and ask him to taste it?

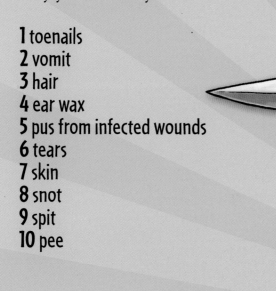

CUT-THROAT CELTS

MOST PEOPLE FIND THEIR HEADS QUITE USEFUL. IT KEEPS THEIR BRAINS FROM FLOPPING ABOUT AND IT GIVES THEIR EYES SOMEWHERE TO SIT. SO IF YOU WANT TO KEEP YOUR HEAD DON'T MAKE A CELT CROSS.

Heads you win, heads you lose

Heads were popular with the Celtic race to which the Britons belonged. Here are ten horrible brainless facts ...

1. In 500 BC, the British tribespeople believed that the head had magical powers. They thought that severed heads could utter prophecies and warnings, especially if they were in groups of three.

2. Rotting human heads were stuck on poles at the entrance to a hill fort.

3. Heads could be thrown into a lake or river as a gift to the gods.

4. After a battle the Celts rode from the battlefield with the heads of enemies dangling from the necks of their horses.

5. The heads might then be nailed to the walls of their houses.

6. Sometimes they were preserved in cedar oil and taken out years later to show off to visitors. A Roman visitor said that the Britons would not part with their lucky heads for their weight in gold.

The Celtic Boii Tribe of the Po Valley (Northern Italy) took skulls and covered them in gold. They would then be used as cups!

CAN'T WE PUT SOME OF THEM OUTSIDE?

8. Heads featured in many ornaments of stone, metal or wood and paintings. Severed heads could be seen staring at you from the surface of tiles, pots, sword hilts, chariot fittings and even bucket handles!

9. Because the gods were more powerful than humans, they often had more heads. An Irish goddess, Ellen, had three heads! The druids had to keep her constantly supplied with sacrifices to stop her coming out of her underworld cave and ravaging the land.

10. The Britons even told stories about the magical power of the head. Many legends involved severed heads. A typical story is the Welsh legend of Bran the Blessed...

DAILY HEADLINE NEWS
HEADITOR : M.T. SKULL

BIG BRAN'S NOGGIN NICKED!

SOME TREACHEROUS TROUBLEMAKER HAS TAKEN BRITAIN'S GREATEST TREASURE!

Yesterday the London burial place of Bran the Blessed was robbed. The great warrior's head was later found to be missing, along with another two skulls from the graveyard. The authorities are looking for a man with three heads!

Magical

As all our readers will know, the head of Bran the Blessed was the most magical article in the whole of Britain. Eight years ago Bran was mortally wounded in a bloody battle with an Irish king. As he lay dying he ordered the seven surviving soldiers to cut off his head and carry it with them. This they did and they found themselves in the afterlife as the guest of Bran – even though they weren't dead!

Then one warrior disobeyed one of Big Bran's orders. He opened a forbidden door. The warriors were heaved out of heaven. But, before they went, one of them tucked Brian's head up his tunic. And so it returned to earth. The head was buried in London, where it would guard Britain against evil for ever more.

Reward

Now it has been stolen there's no knowing what might happen. The Daily Headline News is offering a reward for information leading to its return. Otherwise Britain will be heading for disaster!

VICIOUS VIKINGS

NOBODY IS SURE WHY THE FARMERS OF DENMARK AND NORWAY LEFT THEIR HOMES IN THE 700S AND STARTED RAGING ROUND THE WORLD. BUT YOU DID NOT WANT TO BE ONE OF THEIR VICTIMS.

IVAR THE BONELESS (VIKING, DIED AD 873) VICTIM: KING AELLA

People like horror stories. But the stories aren't always true, even if the people in them really did exist.

 IT ALL STARTED WITH KING AELLA OF NORTHUMBRIA IN ENGLAND. HE KILLED MY DAD. HIS MEN PUSHED HIM IN A PIT OF POISON SNAKES.

SO, THEY SAY ME AND MY BROTHERS CAPTURED AELLA AND TOOK A TERRIBLE REVENGE. FIRST WE TIED HIM TO A TREE...

...THEN WE CUT HIS RIBS AWAY FROM HIS BACKBONE. VERY PAINFUL THAT ... DON'T TRY IT AT HOME.

OUCH

REALLY OUCH

THEN WE RIPPED OUT HIS LUNGS AND SPREAD THEM OVER HIS BACK LIKE THE WINGS OF AN EAGLE.

REALLY REALLY OUCH

REALLY REALLY DEAD

THIS WAS THE FAMOUS BLOOD-EAGLE TORTURE OF THE VIKINGS AND IT TAUGHT AELLA A REAL LESSON! BUT WHY WOULD I GO TO ALL THAT BLEEDING TROUBLE?

Thorgest thumped

The Vikings were supposed to be sneaky and use tricks like ambushes against their enemies. The Irish were supposed to be good sports who liked to fight fairly. But they didn't fight very fair when it came to getting rid of the first Viking chief, Thorgest.

Here's what happened…

Once upon a time there was a lovely Irish girl whose name we don't know. So we won't tell you what it is. Anyway, the Viking warrior Thorgest fell madly in love with the girl and he probably knew her name! 'Let's have a party in my castle tonight, lovely Irish girl. I'll bring a few of my warriors and you bring some of your lovely girl friends to keep them company,' Thorgest said.

'All right, Thorgest,' she said, 'But some of your friends are a bit rough and they'll scare my shy friends. Make sure they leave their weapons behind.'

'I will, lovely Irish girl,' Thorgest said.

So Thorgest turned up with a dozen of his warriors and the lovely Irish girl turned up with a dozen girls. The girls MAY have been lovely too but the Vikings couldn't see their faces. They were hidden behind veils. 'Right, lads,' Thorgest said, 'Start flirting!' But when the Vikings walked up to the girls, the girls threw off their veils and their dresses!! Under those dresses they were Irish warriors with knives. They stuck the knives in the Vikings and killed them all except Thorgest.

The Viking leader was taken to Malachy, the king of Meath, who had him loaded in chains and drowned in a lake.

All because he fell in love with a lovely Irish girl whose name we don't know.

The End

Nice story, but probably just a legend. The massacre didn't do the Irish much good. More Vikings swarmed into Dublin to take thick Thorgest's place.

DREADFUL DARK AGES

WHAT HAPPENS IF YOU ARE LIVING IN THE DARK AGES AND DO SOMETHING NAUGHTY? TOP TIP: 'DO NOT GET CAUGHT.' OTHERWISE YOU MIGHT MEET ONE OF MY FIENDISH FRIENDS.

The Dark Ages (around AD 400–1000) are sometimes thought of as 'lawless'. When the Romans left Britain, the Angles and Saxons invaded. Then the Vikings began to rampage around Europe murdering monks, flattening farmers, bashing babies and terrorizing towns. But the deadly Dark Ages did have their own methods of punishment…

ALFRED THE GREAT? I'M ALFRED THE BLOOMIN' MARVELLOUS!

Artful Alfred

King Alfred ruled Britain from 871 till 901. He took all the old laws and organized them into a new book of laws for the Saxons.

There were ways of finding out if a person was guilty of a crime. They were called 'ordeals'. If you passed through the ordeal you were innocent – but if you failed you were guilty … and you suffered from both the test and then a punishment.

1. Ordeal by cake: A special cake is baked. The victim has to swear, 'If I did this crime then may this cake choke me!' and eat the cake. Sounds harmless enough, but Earl Godwin was banished from England for disobeying the good King Edward – a year later Godwin returned and declared…

PEOPLE SAY I KILLED YOUR BROTHER. BUT, IF THAT IS TRUE, THEN MAY GOD LET THIS PIECE OF BREAD CHOKE ME.

ME AND MY BIG MOUTH!

A minute later Godwin was dead. He had choked on the piece of bread!

2. Ordeal by cold water: The accused is tied hand and foot. A rope is placed around them and they are lowered into a pool. If they sink then they are innocent… and if they float then they are guilty. (This test was still being used in the 17th century to test people accused of being witches! More about that later…)

3. Ordeal by hot water: The accused must plunge a bare arm into a pot of hot water and pull out a stone at the bottom of the pot. The arm will then be bandaged for three days. At the end of three days the bandage will be taken off. If the arm is healed then they are innocent … but, if there is still a scald, they are guilty and must be punished.

4. Ordeal by hot metal: The accused must grip a hot iron rod and walk with it for a set distance. Again the hand is bandaged for three days and the wound examined.

5. Ordeal by combat: If two people argue about who owns a brooch or a piece of land (or a stale cheese sandwich) then they have a fight. The winner of the fight is judged to be the lawful owner. Actually, this still goes on in schools today!

6. Ordeal by lot: Try this in your own classroom!

YOU NEED:
Three sticks labelled 'GUILTY', 'NOT GUILTY' and 'TRINITY'. (The sticks used in iced lollies are best.)
A treasure (at least 2p and maybe as much as 5p).

TO WORK:
1 Select three people to be 'Suspects' and one to be the 'Judge'.
2 The judge places the treasure on the table and turns his or her back.
3 One of the suspects steals the treasure.
4 The judge blindfolds each suspect in turn and asks each one to pick a stick.

The suspect then gives back the stick to the judge.
5 The verdict: a) Pick 'Guilty' and you are guilty.
  b) Pick 'Not guilty' and you are free to go.
  c) Pick 'Trinity' and you must pick another stick.
6 Of course all three could pick 'Guilty' or all three could be 'Not guilty'.
Hard luck, judge. Try again until you get just one guilty person.

Try it. Does it work? It's not as painful as trial by boiling water but you could be found guilty just by picking the wrong stick. Good idea for football matches though - better than a penalty shoot-out.

NASTY NORMANS

THE NORMANS WERE VIKINGS WHO HAD MOVED TO THE NORTH OF FRANCE. THEIR KNIGHTS WERE ALWAYS GREEDY FOR MORE LAND. THEY ENDED UP IN ENGLAND AND WALES. HOW DID THEY GET SO POWERFUL? BY CHEATING. NEVER TRUST A NORMAN KNIGHT...

Awful at Abergavenny

In 1175 one of the nastiest Norman deeds was done at Abergavenny Castle. The Norman lord, William de Braose, was having a feast. A Christmas feast! How jolly. He invited the Welsh chieftain of Gwent, Seisyll. How kind. Especially as it was Seisyll who had murdered William de Braose's Uncle Henry.

William had a very special Christmas present for Seisyll. If there had been newspapers in those days then it would have made the front page.

Abergavenny Advertiser

FREE! ILLUMINATED MANUSCRIPT WITH THE Advertiser on Sunday

SILENT KNIGHTS!

'Tis the season to be jolly or ... in the case of William de Braose ... jolly vicious.

Our Norman lord sent out invitations to his old Welsh enemy, Seisyll the chieftain of Gwent.

'Bring your son and his son Gruffydd, and your top knights,' wily William wrote. 'We'll have a great knight out!' he joked.

The Welsh arrived and took off their weapons – those wonderful Welsh, it's good manners to do that. And then they started drinking and eating.

A servant at Abergavenny Castle said this morning,

'There was more drinking than eating. Well, to tell the truth it was the Welsh doing all the drinking – William and the Normans just sipped a little watered wine.'

As midnight struck so did the Normans[1]! First Lord William told his guests, 'I have made a new law that says no Welsh man will ever be allowed to carry a weapon in my lands again.'

Seisyll cried, 'You can never make us obey that, de Braose!' and that's just what the nifty Norman was waiting to hear.

'You've refused to obey an order from the king,' William roared. 'That's treason. The punishment is death. Normans! Kill, them!'

That's when the Normans drew their weapons and hacked Seisyll and his knights to pieces. The only Christmas boxes they'll be getting are wooden boxes to bury them in!

But William's revenge was not complete. William chased Seisyll's wife Gwladus as she tried to escape.

She tried to shield her seven-year-old son in her arms. He was hacked to death.

'Blood all over the rushes on the floor,' our servant said. 'Blood and body bits. We'll have to throw out all the rushes and bury the bodies. We was hoping for a holiday. Some Christmas this has turned out to be!'

William de Braose became known as the 'Ogre of Abergavenny'.

1. Oh, all right, clocks hadn't been invented in those days. Midnight didn't 'strike'. They probably used candles to mark off the hours. If you really want to be fussy let's say, 'As midnight dripped its wax …'

Bill's last battle

William was back in France, attacking the town of Mantes, when he had his last illness. He'd had the town burned to the ground and (one story says) his horse was frightened by the shower of sparks.

The horse stumbled, William slammed his stomach against the front of his saddle and burst his fat gut. He died five weeks later after suffering in agony. Before he died he handed his crown and sword to his son William Rufus. But the moment he died the Norman lords panicked. With the Conqueror dead there could be rebellions in their lands.

Orderic Vitalis, writing 50 years after the death, described what happened next…

As soon as William died, the richest of the Norman lords mounted their horses and hurried off to defend their castles. The servants – seeing that their masters had disappeared – laid their hands on the weapons, the gold and silver plate, the rich cloth and the royal furniture. The corpse of the king was left almost naked on the floor.

The disappearing conqueror

William's body was eventually taken to Caen to be buried in the cathedral William had founded. The journey to the church was interrupted by a fire in the town – they dropped the body, fought the fire, then carried on.

Later the funeral service was interrupted by a local man who said…

THE GROUND WHERE YOU'RE BURYING WILLIAM BELONGS TO ME! I WANT TO BE PAID BEFORE YOU PUT HIM IN THE GRAVE!

He was paid!

Then the clumsy undertakers tried to cram the fat body into a small stone coffin and bits fell off. The smell was so disgusting the bishop rushed through the burial service and everyone ran for it.

Rest in peace, William? No. Only until 1522. In that year the curious Catholic Church had the tomb opened to inspect the body.

Rest in peace, William? No. Only until 1562. In that year Protestants raided the church, broke open tombs and scattered skeletons. All that was left was Will's thigh bone. That was re-buried and a fine monument was built.

Rest in peace, William's thigh bone? No. Only until 1792 when the French Revolution mobs demolished his monument.

Rest in peace, William? For the moment. A simple stone slab now marks the spot where he was buried.

But what happened to that thigh bone? Some say the 1792 rioters threw it out – some say it's still there. Perhaps someone should open the tomb again and find out!

OVER MY DEAD BODY!

Wicked Warriors

An executioner is paid to kill criminals. We don't do it for fun. But there were people who enjoyed killing other people. Keep away from warriors or it may be your top for the chop-a-lop.

Sword-swishing samurai
Savage sword-swishers who severed several heads

Place: Japan. Time: 400s to 1800s

These Japanese warriors used horses and armour in the 400s, long before the Normans and the knights of Europe came along.

Then, in AD 1192 Yoritomo became the first Shogun of Japan and set up his samurai knights as lords of the people.

They went on bossing Japan until the 1800s, long after 'knight' was just a title in Europe.
They were trained to be fearless and true to their lord, the Shogun.

At first they used bows and arrows with swords just for lopping off enemy heads. By the 1200s they started to use spears. They also spent more time fighting on foot, using two swords.

Now for the HORRIBLE history…

This test report would be a bit more interesting than your school test report of course.

You only get, 'Can do better' but samurai swords got 'Can cut butter'.

You get, 'Nice handwriting' but samurai swords got 'Nice hand-slicing'.

Now for the REALLY HORRIBLE history… The swords would sometimes be tested on live criminals who were waiting to be executed. Instead of a fast finish they died a little bit at a time.

In 1876, Emperor Meiji made a new law that ended the wearing of swords. The samurai had lost their jobs – criminals kept their fingers and toes.

Kids get killed too

In 1185, at the Battle of Dan-no-ura, the samurai knights of Minamoto Yoritomo attacked the fleet of the Emperor of Japan. The Emperor was just six years old.

When the battle was lost the Emperor's granny threw him off the boat and drowned him to save him from Minamoto Yoritomo and his samurai.

Even today some Japanese believe the crabs hold the spirits of the dead warriors. Poor crab!

MARTIN BROWN'S BEASTLY BEST BITS

MEASLY MIDDLE AGES

I COULD GO ROUND CUTTING OFF HEADS TILL MY ARMS WERE TOO TIRED TO EVEN CHOP A CHIP. BUT THE WORLD HAS SEEN MORE DEADLY KILLERS THAN ME. KILLERS SO SMALL YOU CAN HARDLY SEE THEM.

Dreadful disease

In 1347, Death strolled through Europe with his scythe, mowing some down and missing others. Swish! Swish! In 1349, he sailed across the Channel to the British Isles. The terrified people never knew who was going to be next. As an Italian diary recorded…

> There appeared certain swellings in the groin and under the armpit, the victims spat blood, and in three days they were dead

These swellings began to ooze with blood and pus. Purple-black blotches appeared on the skin and you smelled absolutely revolting!

Swell – Spit – Smell – Swish! You were gone.

Death's 'scythe' was the bubonic plague and the piles of bodies grew like chopped straw into a haystack. They were loaded on to carts, dropped into pits – or, in Avignon in France, thrown in the river.

Children were Death's particular favourites when it came to the swish. We now know the real reason for this: if you are an adult then you have had quite a few diseases in your lifetime and build up a 'resistance'; children have had fewer diseases and far less resistance. They die easily.

Of course, preachers said the children probably got what they deserved! One explained…

> It may be that children suffer heaven's revenge because they miss going to church or because they despise their fathers and mothers. God kills children with the plague as you can see every day – because, according to the old law, children who are rebels (or disobedient to their parents) are punished by death.

You can see that not much has changed.

Crazy cures

The trouble was that doctors didn't know what caused the plague and they didn't know how to cure it. People mistakenly believed you could catch it by looking at a victim, breathing bad air drinking from poisoned wells.

In France they said the English did the poisoning, in Spain they blamed the Arabs. In Germany, suspected poisoners were nailed into barrels and thrown into the river. And everyone blamed lepers!

And the cures were almost as dreadful as

the disease. Doctors already had some wacky cures for illnesses. They said…

✸ wear a magpie's beak around the neck to cure toothache

✸ cut a hole in the skull to let out the devil and cure madness.

With something as deadly as the bubonic plague they had no chance! They suggested…

✸ throw sweet-smelling herbs on a fire to clean the air

✸ sit in a sewer so the bad air of the plague is driven off by the worse air of the drains

PERHAPS THE PLAGUE'S NOT SO BAD AFTER ALL

✸ drink a medicine of ten-year-old treacle

✸ swallow powders of crushed emeralds (for the rich)

✸ eat arsenic powder (highly poisonous!)

✸ try letting blood out of the patient (when the patient's horoscope was right!)

✸ kill all the cats and dogs in the town

✸ shave a live chicken's bottom and strap it to the plague sore

IT'S BAD ENOUGH THAT I'M DYING WITHOUT LOOKING STUPID TOO

✸ march from town to town flogging yourself with a whip.

The doctors checked the urine of their patients. If there was blood in it then there was no hope.

Some people who caught the plague had a natural resistance to it so they recovered. Others took the only 'cure' that worked – run away from the plague-infested towns into the countryside. The rich people, with country houses, could do this. The poor stayed at home and died.

The real cause of the plague wasn't discovered till just a hundred years ago. And people still don't understand – they think rats carried the plague. Fleas carried the plague germs. They lived on rats and their germs killed the rats.

A dead rat is not very tasty (as children who stay to school dinners will tell you) so the fleas looked for a new 'home'. If there were no rats about then the fleas would hop on to a human and spread the germs to that human. When their new human friend died they'd hop on to another human – maybe the person who'd nursed the first victim. And so it went on.

I THINK I'VE GOT FLEAS DAD

ALL THIS PLAGUE AROUND AND YOU'RE WORRIED ABOUT A FEW FLEAS

SCRATCH SCRATCH

AWFUL FOR ANIMALS

HISTORY HAS BEEN HORRIBLE TO ANIMALS AS WELL AS PEOPLE. FOR HUNDREDS OF YEARS GREAT CITIES LIKE LONDON MADE CRUELTY INTO 'SPORT' FOR PEOPLE TO WATCH.

In prehistoric times – before London was built – there must have been sharks in Soho and wolves in Wapping, crocodiles snapping in Shoreditch and hyenas – who probably just came for a good laugh.

Then London was built. London has been a horrible place for many humans. It has also been awful for animals.

There was…

Bear-baiting

London had bear-gardens since the time of Henry II (1154–1189). A bear would have its teeth and claws removed, then it was chained to a post by a back leg or by the neck. Trained dogs were sent to attack it. This was called 'baiting'.

The Dutch scholar Erasmus, writing about 1500, said…

There are many herds of bears kept in England just to be baited. Sunday is the favourite day for these sports.

ARE WE A HERD?

FIRST I'VE HEARD

Hentzner, a German traveller writing in 1598, described the bear-garden at Bankside in London as a sort of a theatre for the baiting of bulls and bears.

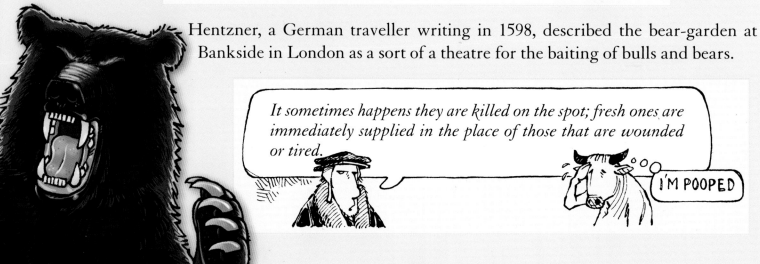

It sometimes happens they are killed on the spot; fresh ones are immediately supplied in the place of those that are wounded or tired.

I'M POOPED

He also describes the whipping of a blinded bear for 'fun'.

A famous baiting took place before Queen Elizabeth in 1575, for which 13 bears were provided. Richard Laneham was amongst the guests. He wrote:

> *It was a very pleasant sport to see. To see the bear, with his pink eyes, tearing after his enemies; the nimbleness and cunning of the dog against the strength and experience of the bear: if he were bitten then see him get free with biting, with clawing, with roaring, with tossing and tumbling; and when he was loose to shake his ears two or three times with the blood and the slaver hanging about his face.*

Bull-baiting

It wasn't just bears that suffered and died in the bear-pits of London. Bulls did too. A hundred years after Elizabeth baited her last bear it was still going on … but not everyone enjoyed it so much. Some even felt sorry for the animals. John Evelyn wrote in his now-famous Diary in 1670:

> *I went with some friends to the bear-garden, where there was cock-fighting, dog-fighting, bear and bull-baiting, it being a famous day for all these butcherly sports, or rather barbarous cruelties. The bulls did exceedingly well, but the Irish wolf-dog was best when it beat a cruel mastiff. One of the bulls tossed a dog into a lady's lap, as she sat in one of the boxes quite high above the arena. Two poor dogs were killed, and it all ended with the ape on horseback. I am most heartily weary of these crude and dirty pastimes.*

By the 1800s people were trying to ban these sports. But when Tsar Nicholas I of Russia visited England he was taken to see a bull-baiting.

The bull's nose was blown full of pepper to drive it wild. Tricks to make a bear mad included putting dried peas in its ear or tying fireworks to its back.

Bear-baiting and bull-baiting were banned by law in 1835. Many people ignored the ban and went ahead anyway. There was a bull-baiting event at London's Agricultural Hall in 1870.

So much for the law.

Cock-fighting

Cock-fighting was banned in 1849 (but still goes on in London, in secret, today). Sometimes fighting cockerels are pecked to death. Sometimes their hearts are stabbed by sharp spurs fastened to claws.

Dog-fighting

Dog-fighting was also banned but still goes on today. In London in the 1800s you could get advice on how to train your dog to kill … and win fights and make you money.

A writer in the 1850s complained you couldn't get to see many dog-fights in pubs, like you could in the old days. But there were plenty of dog-fights in the homes of rich men, where they were hidden from the law.

Horse and pony-baiting

From time to time there was horse-baiting in London. On one occasion the horse actually won. The crowd was furious and tore tiles off the roof of the theatre till the horse was brought back and attacked by more dogs.

The crowd wasn't happy till the horse was dead.

The Paris Garden in Southwark was the chief bear-garden in London. A Spanish nobleman of the 1580s was taken to see a pony baited. The pony had an ape tied to its back.

> *The animal was kicking amongst the dogs, while the ape clung to its back and screamed. The dogs hung from the ears and neck of the pony. It was very laughable.*

We do not know what the pony thought of it.

In 1790 a pony was trained to kill sheep for 'sport'. The report said…

> *The pony seized a sheep and bit and kicked it till it died. It then separated the head from the neck and ate nearly two quarters of the sheep.*

Today this sort of thing would get you barred from the Pony Club. (Or baa-ed.)

Badger-baiting

When bear-baiting became illegal some cruel London 'sportsmen' turned to killing badgers with dogs. In the 1700s they would nail a badger's tail to the floor then set dogs to kill it.

Bad for bunnies

Regent's Park Zoo is a popular place to visit in London. In the 1870s you could see the boa constrictor snake being fed … with a live rabbit. The writer William Thackeray was horrified. He said…

> *Yes — swallowing a live rabbit, sir, and looking as if he would have swallowed one of my little children after it.*

That would stop them rabbitting on.

Ruthless Rulers

DO TRY TO BE A RULER WHEN YOU GO BACK IN TIME. IT IS USUALLY THE RULER THAT GIVES THE EXECUTIONERS THE ORDERS. YOU CAN INVENT SOME HORRIBLY HISTORICAL WAYS TO FINISH OFF YOUR FOES ... AND FRIENDS.

Tsar Peter III of Russia discovered that his wife Catherine had a boyfriend. He had the boyfriend's head chopped off and put in a jar. Catherine was then forced to have the jar at her bedside wherever she went. That is Rotten Ruling.

If you are going to be a Rotten Ruler you need to think of new ways to kill people. People will remember you if you do that. Get the idea? Go and think of your own ways to kill people. Here are some examples to give you some ideas.

Emperor Alexander Severus of Rome (ruled AD 222–135)

Emperor Elagabalus planned to have his nephew Alexander killed. But Alexander's friends started killing off Elagabalus's assassins first.

They didn't just chop them up or poison them. They made sure they died slowly. They held them down, slit them open, then pulled out their guts, their livers, their lungs and their hearts.

Sultan Selim II of Turkey (ruled 1566–1574)

Selim loved booze. He really, really loved Cyprus wine. But one day he ran out of his favourite tipple.

Horror! 'What can I do to get some more?' he whined.

'Take over Cyprus,' his friends told him.

So he invaded Cyprus. Thirty thousand people died in the battles.

Finally the leader of the Cypriot army, Bragadino, was captured. He was skinned alive. His skin was stuffed with straw and paraded in front of the troops from Turkey.

Genghis Khan of Mongolia (1167–1227)

Mongol warlord Genghis Khan won a battle then discovered that the enemy warlord was an old friend. He said:

And that's what they did.

Robert III of Scotland
(1337–1406)

Robert had a lot of trouble with Scottish clans, who wouldn't stop fighting. To solve the problem he came up with a clever idea.

In 1396 he organized a contest on the North Inch of Perth. Robert and a huge crowd watched as 30 men of the Clan Davidson fought against 30 men of the MacPherson clan.

The fight was to the death.

Each man was dressed in a short kilt and armed with sword, dagger, axe, crossbow and three arrows.

Bagpipes played and the men slaughtered each other until at the end of the day only a dozen were still alive.

They were all badly wounded.

Of course the dead and wounded had been the worst troublemakers in Scotland. After that it was much more peaceful in the Scottish Highlands.

Emperor Tiberius of Rome
(ruled AD 14–37)

This bad-tempered man was easily upset. And if you upset him he'd have your ears cut off and fed to his lions.

He became so annoyed with one of his wives that he had her locked in the bathroom, then ordered his servants to turn up the heat.

She was steamed to death.

Emperor Wenceslas of Germany
(ruled 1378–1400)

Wenceslas was angry with his chef for cooking him a mouldy meal. The Emperor ordered him to be executed. The chef was taken away and roasted alive on his own kitchen spit.

ANGRY AZTECS

IN MEXICO AROUND 1300 TO 1500 THE TERRORS OF THE TIME WERE THE AZTEC PEOPLE. OF ALL THE HORRIBLES IN HISTORY THE AZTECS COME CLOSE TO THE TOP OF THE PILE. FAR WORSE THAN CHEERFUL CHOPPERS LIKE ME. LOOK AT THEIR HORRIBLE HOBBY OF SACRIFICING HUMANS...

The good gore guide

You know that the sun is a star ... a large celestial body composed of gravitationally contained hot gases emitting electromagnetic radiation, especially light, as a result of nuclear reactions inside the star. (No, I don't understand what it means either but it sounds good if you say it quickly.)

Anyway the Toltecs believed it was actually a god. A superhuman being who has power over human life.

Now these god people can be very tricky. If you upset them then they'll make you suffer – shine too hot on your crops, shrivel them up and starve you, or send a plague of locusts to eat all your food. The thing to do is keep your god (or gods) happy.

Some people think their god will be happy with a bit of praise and a few hymns and prayers. Other people believe they have to give prezzies to their god.

The terrible Toltecs believed you had to give a life to their god – a sacrifice.

But the awful aztecs took it to extremes. They believed they had to give their sun god human lives – thousands of them. And, not only that, they had to be sacrificed in a gruesomely gory way.

1. FIRST CHOOSE YOUR VICTIM

IT COULD BE YOU!

OOOH! I WONDER WHAT I WON?

2. TAKE THEM UP THE STEPS TO THE TOP OF THE PYRAMID

PHEW! I'LL BE DEAD BY THE TIME I REACH THE TOP!

I HOPE NOT

3. TIE THE VICTIM ON A CURVED ALTAR

YOU'RE A MAN AFTER MY OWN HEART

THAT'S TRUE

4. TAKE AN OBSIDIAN KNIFE AND CAREFULLY OPEN THE CHEST

LETS OPEN THE CHEST, SHALL WE?

THIS MUST BE MY TREASURE CHEST! AT LAST, MY PRIZE!

The Aztecs didn't sacrifice the odd human on special occasions like the king's birthday or Bank Holiday Mondays. They did it all the time. They…

✹ sacrificed 50,000 a year (that's a thousand a week, six an hour or one every ten minutes!)

✹ sacrificed 20,000 in a single party when they opened the temple at Tenochtitlan

✹ had an army specially organized to keep the priests supplied with victims

✹ stirred up trouble among the conquered tribes so they had an excuse to go in and take prisoners who became sacrifice victims.

A Spanish history book said that when the Great Temple was opened in 1487 there were 80,000 victims sacrificed in one ceremony. But don't believe everything you read in history books! Because sacrificing 80,000 would have been just about impossible! The Aztecs would have needed machine guns and bombs to massacre that many. (In fact it's only in the past hundred years that humans have learned to kill each other at that rate – but modern people call it war and that makes it all right.)

Knasty Knights

IN THE MIDDLE AGES KNIGHTS WENT AROUND BASHING PEOPLE IN BATTLE. BUT THAT WAS FINE BECAUSE GOD SAID IT WAS OK TO KILL PEOPLE WHO WEREN'T CHRISTIAN. DO NOT ARGUE WITH A MAN IN AN ARMOUR CAN ... UNLESS YOU HAVE A MACHINE GUN.

Crazy Christians

Blame Gregory the Great! Early Christians believed that war was evil and Christians shouldn't fight. Then Gregory became Pope in AD 590 and said…

1) THERE ARE NON-CHRISTIANS OUT THERE WHO NEED TO BE CONVERTED

WHAT IF THEY DON'T WANT TO BECOME CHRISTIANS YOUR HOLINESS?

2) FORCE THEM! GO TO WAR WITH THEM! THREATEN THEM!

WHAT IF THEY STILL REFUSE, YOUR HOLY NUTS?

3) YOU'LL JUST HAVE TO KILL THEM AND GO ON KILLING THEM TILL THEY SEE SENSE

WHAT IF THEY KILL US FIRST, YOUR HOOLIGUTS?

4) THEN YOU WILL GO STRAIGHT TO HEAVEN, WON'T YOU?

LET'S GO AND PUT THE BOOT IN THE UNBELIEVERS, LADS!

CLANG!

BANG

TWANG

STAB

BLEED

GRRR

Of course, bishops were not allowed to spill blood – even heathen blood – so they went into battle with dirty great clubs called 'maces'. With a mace they could bash a non-Christian on the bonce and kill him without spilling a drop. Two Popes even went off to battle with their armies. A new Christian belief grew: 'Love thy neighbour … but you may need to batter him over the head with a stick if he doesn't have the same beliefs as you.'

When knights came along five hundred years after Greg the Great they had a perfect excuse for fighting. It was a war against enemies of the Christian religion and it was known as a Crusade…

Terrible Turk talk

In 1095, Pope Urban II decided it was time the Christians took over Jerusalem. It was their Holy City and was full of Turks, who were Muslims. Unfortunately it was also a Holy City to the Muslims and they weren't going to give it up without a fight.

The Pope's priests needed men with swords to drive the Turks out of the city so he sent an invitation to knights to fight for their Christian church.

The Pope didn't send out letters asking for volunteers. He stood on a platform and announced that he wanted Christians to fight against the Turks. He then did the old warmaker's trick of telling people how rotten the enemy was. Urban said…

The Turks cut open the navels of Christians that they want to torment with a loathsome death. They tear out their organs and tie them to a stake. They drag their victims round the stake and flog them. They kill them as they lie flat on the ground with their entrails out. They tie some to posts and shoot them full of arrows. They order others to bare their necks and attack them with swords trying to see if they can cut off their heads with a single stroke.

And you thought your history teacher was tough!

THERE'S A FIGHT ON THE BATTLEMENTS!

OR A BATTLE ON THE FIGHTLEMENTS?

ARGH

PENK

PING!

THUD!

ERK

?

TERRIFYING TUDORS

THE TUDOR FAMILY RULED ENGLAND FROM 1485 TILL 1603. IF YOU WANTED TO SURVIVE THE TOP TIP HAS TO BE, 'DO NOT MARRY KING HENRY VIII.' MIND YOU, HE WAS A GREAT BLOKE TO WORK FOR AND KEPT THE EXECUTIONERS REALLY BUSY.

Beheaded Boleyn

The Queen of England from 1533 till 1536, Anne was largely hated by the English people. King Henry VIII made sure she was remembered as wicked even though he had poor Anne beheaded. That's how HIS-story can twist things…

Win a pig! p.17

THE TUDOR TIMES

Friday 19 May 1536

GOGGLE EYES GETS IT IN THE NECK

At 8 a.m. this morning King Henry VIII's ex-wife, the witch Anne Boleyn, died when her head hit the straw at the Tower of London. She had been charged with treason and everyone knew she was guilty.

Ms Boleyn was known for her plain face and her bad temper. As well as her goggle eyes, her mouth was too wide and her skin too dull. The proof that she was a witch lay in the fact that she had six fingers on one hand and a large wart under her chin. Clearly Good King Henry was under one of her spells when he married her!

Today an imported French swordsman took off her head with a single blow. It is said that her heart was stolen from her body to be hidden near her home in Norfolk.

Anne Boleyn going on her 'chopping' trip.

Anne was almost certainly NOT guilty of any crime. Henry was simply annoyed with her for not providing him with any sons. It is said that her ghost can be seen – with her head on her lap – at Blickling Hall in Norfolk.

Foul fact

Anne Boleyn had an eating disorder. She would very often eat a meal … then be sick before she could leave the table. Her ladies-in-waiting became used to this and would hold up a sheet in front of her while she vomited into a bowl. Of course, Henry was supposed to have written the song, Greensleeves. Was it inspired by Anne's sickness? And could Henry have added a verse like…

Alas, my love, you are looking bad;
Perhaps it's the mouldy old peas you had.
I used to love the white dress, it is sad,
Because since you've been sick it's got green sleeves!

Fantastic fact

Anne Boleyn's head was cut off quickly and cleanly while she prayed. So quickly, in fact, that it is said her lips moved after her head was severed.

Funny fact

Henry had six wives. But not many people know that wife number six (Catherine Parr) had four husbands of her own including Henry.

Mean queen

Everyone knows about Henry's bloodthirsty nature. But they forget about his wives' nasty little habits. For example, Catherine of Aragon was left in charge of England while Henry went over to France. While he was away, Catherine's armies fought the Scottish king, James IV, and beat him at the battle of Flodden Field. Just to prove what a clever girl she was, Cathy sent Henry the blood-stained coat of the dead Scottish king.

Not-so-mean queen

Rumour said that wife number two (Anne Boleyn) poisoned wife number one (Catherine of Aragon). But people would say that … Catherine was popular – Anne wasn't. In fact, when Anne went to her coronation in a fine procession, people crowded the London streets to see her – but no one cheered. The doctor's report on Catherine's body describes something more like cancer. So, it's 'Not guilty, Anne.'

EXCELLENT EXECUTIONERS

EVERYBODY THINKS, 'OOOOH! IT MUST BE AWFUL TO HAVE YOUR HEAD CUT OFF.' NOBODY EVER THINKS, 'OOOOH! IT MUST BE AWFUL TO CUT SOMEONE'S HEAD OFF.' IT'S ABOUT TIME YOU DID. I'M AXING YOU TO SEE IT FROM MY POINT OF VIEW.

Lottery of life losers

Margaret Pole, Countess of Salisbury – 1541
What would *you* do if an executioner said...

RIGHT MATE, LET'S HAVE YOUR NECK ON THIS CHOPPING BLOCK

Would you do as you were told? Would you say, as you were supposed to, 'I forgive you, executioner,' and give him a bag of gold? Or would you be really rotten to the poor axeman, like the eccentric old Countess of Salisbury?

Henry VIII planned to visit York. He wanted the Tower of London empty of prisoners so none would escape while his back was turned. One of those prisoners was the Countess of Salisbury. When it was her turn to be executed, Henry's chief executioner, Master Cratwell, was away from London. The job was left to a boy. You have to feel sorry for him!

If the young executioner had written a letter home then it might have looked something like this...

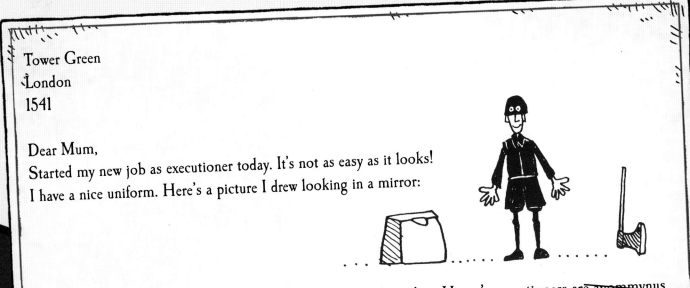

Tower Green
London
1541

Dear Mum,
Started my new job as executioner today. It's not as easy as it looks!
I have a nice uniform. Here's a picture I drew looking in a mirror:

You'd be proud of me – except you wouldn't know it was me 'cos Henry's executioners are ~~anommynus~~ ~~annunnymous~~ secret.

Anyway, the boss, Robert Cratwell (whose name I can't tell you 'cos it's secret), said I could start with an easy one. 'It's the old Countess of Salisbury,' he said. 'She's nearly 70 years old so she'll be no trouble.'

'Seventy!' I said. 'If she gets any older her head'll probably just drop off!' I laughed. I didn't know the joke would be on me! 'What's the old trout done?' I asked.

'Nothing,' Robert said. 'She's never had a trial or been found guilty. But her son, Cardinal Pole, was a Catholic and he started stirring up trouble for the King. So Henry had the Cardinal's old mother thrown in the Tower a couple of years ago. And the King made sure she suffered in there with terrible food and no heating. The old woman will be glad to be out of it.'

Then he gave me a few last-minute lessons in chopping and sent me off to do some target-practice on a turnip. I was spot on. That turnip was sliced as neat as one that you'd put in your stew, Mum. But there was no one watching, was there? And turnips don't move.

Imagine the shock when I found dozens of people gathered round the scaffold! I was shaking with nerves, I can tell you. 'Would you mind putting your head on the block?' I asked her, ever so polite, just the way you taught me.

Blow me, but the old woman said, 'No! A traitor would put their head on the block, but I'm not a traitor, so I won't!'

Her two guards grabbed her and held her down on her knees. But she was struggling all the time. They couldn't hold her head down because I'd have cut their hands off. That meant she could still move her head around. Then she looked up at me and said, 'Catch me if you can.' She started bobbing and weaving and I started chopping. Well, I made a right mess of her shoulders before I finally got her in the neck and finished her off.

It was my job to hold up the head and cry, 'Behold the head of a traitor!' I was that scared I think I said, 'Behold the head of a tater!' The witnesses were booing and throwing things at me. It was awful, Mum.

But Robert's back now and I'm getting extra lessons. In the meantime I'm working away in the torture chamber. They don't mind if you're clumsy in there and you don't have a big audience.

Give my love to the kids and the cat. I'll be home next week to help with chopping the firewood.

Love,
Your little Georgie

We don't know what happened to the boy executioner – but his master, Cratwell, was later hanged for robbery!

INCREDIBLE INCA

IT DOESN'T MATTER WHAT AGE YOU LIVE IN. IT IS NOT A GOOD IDEA TO BE A WOMAN. TAKE THE INCA PEOPLE WHO LIVED IN PERU IN THE MIDDLE AGES. YOU DO NOT WANT TO BE A WOMAN THERE...

Cheerless chosen women

Would you like to be an Incan 'Chosen Woman'? Sounds a bit special, doesn't it? If the Incas had advertised for Chosen Women they might have done it like this:

By the 1500s there were several thousand of these Chosen Women. Would you apply?

GIRLS!
THE CHANCE OF A LIFETIME!
Why don't YOU apply to be a
QUECHUA ACLLA CUNA
— that's right, a CHOSEN WOMAN!

GET TO LIVE IN THE TEMPLE!

NO MEN TO BOTHER YOU!

SIMPLE TASKS INCLUDE:
🌙 COOK THE HOLY FOOD. ☉ KEEP THE SACRED FIRE GOING.
◎ WEAVE THE EMPEROR'S TEMPLE CLOTHES.

ALL YOU NEED IS TO BE BEAUTIFUL AND CLEVER
AND AGED BETWEEN 8 AND 10 YEARS!

STAY SHUT UP FOR AT LEAST SIX HAPPY YEARS!

THE LUCKY ONES WILL LEAVE TO MARRY LORDS! *

Apply to the matron (Mama Cuna) of your local temple or the High Priestess (Coya Pasca) — the wife of the Sun god himself!

*The really lucky ones will end up as a temple sacrifice, of course.

Wee women

Girls! Want to look like an Incan woman? You'll need to dress your hair like the Incas. Here's how to do it…

1. Collect pee in a bucket. (Your family and friends can all chip in and help you fill that bucket fast.)

2. Leave the pee for a week to brew (the way beer is left to brew – except your pee won't end up tasting like brown ale).

3. Wash your hair by soaking it in the bucket of brewed pee. (This will get rid of the grease and leave your hair lovely and shiny – honest!)

SPLISH

PLITCH PLITCH

4. When your hair is dry you can start making it into braids. To hold the hair in place wet it with some of that pee. (Hair spray hasn't been invented. Sorry.)

5. Find your Prince Charming and say…

HIYA HANDSOME! WOULD YOU LIKE TO RUN YOUR FINGERS THROUGH MY HAIR?

Then hope that your Prince Charming likes a Cinderella who smells like a toilet!

INCA STINKA

SUPER SHAKESPEARE

People went to plays to see the characters murder each other, shed buckets of stage-blood and even eat each other!

Shakespeare's bloodiest play of all was *Macbeth*. Here's a short extract to show how brilliant – and how totally tasteless – Will Shakespeare could be. Warning: this play contains scenes of violence that some people may find upsetting.

MACBETH

by William Shakespeare and A.N. Other

IMPORTANT NOTE: All the words in italics in this script were written by Shakespeare (honest!). All the words written in normal type are by A.N. Other.

Scene 4 Macduff's castle

Narrator: Macbeth was a nasty man who killed the king and took his throne. Then he set out to kill his other enemies ... especially the noble Macduff. First he sent a couple of murderers to Macduff's castle ...

Murderer: *Where is your husband?*
Lady Macduff: *In no such place as thou may find him.*
Murderer: *He is a traitor.*
Young Macduff: *Thou liest, thou shag-haired villain!*
Murderer: *What, you egg!*
(And the murderer stabs young Macduff)

Young Macduff: *He has killed me, mother.* (Yes. This line really is in the printed play. But it's hard to believe witty Will really wrote it.) *Run away, I pray you!*
(Lady Macduff runs away, chased by the murderer. Screams off stage tell us that he caught her.)

Lady Macduff: Help! They've caught me! Ouch!

Narrator: When Macduff heard about his family's death, he came back home to Scotland for revenge! Macbeth was left to face Macduff alone ...
(Macduff enters waving a sword)

Macduff: *Tyrant, show thy face!*

Macbeth: *Of all men else I have avoided thee,*
My soul is too much charged with blood of thine.

Macduff: *I have no words;*
My voice is in my sword.
(They fight and Macduff kills Macbeth)

Narrator: And so Macduff killed Macbeth.

Macbeth: I guess that serves me right.

Macduff: So, that's the end of rotten old Macbeth.
And now it's to the pub to celebrate!

Narrator: The end!

SLIMY STUARTS

'THE BLACK DEATH' COULD KILL BY THE MILLION IN THE MIDDLE AGES. BUT IT WAS STILL JUST AS DANGEROUS IN THE TIMES OF THE SLIMY STUART MONARCHS OF THE 1600S. SPOT IT OR DIE.

Fire and plague

Londoners who lived through Charles II's reign were pretty lucky ... lucky that the plague didn't get them! And if the plague spared their lives then the Great Fire probably destroyed their houses. Would you have survived in Stuart London?

The plague ... read all about it!

PENNY FOR THE GUY

9th Sept 1665 — *PLAGUE WEEKLY* — ON THE SPOTS REPORTS — Only 2OP WEEKLY

BOOZY BARD BEDEVILS BURIAL BOYS

Last night the brave burial boys, who collect your old corpses, were almost scared to death themselves. A strolling singer sat up and spooked them just as they were about to pop him in the pit.

DIRTY

Corpse collector Samuel Simple (34 or 37) said, 'It's a dirty job but somebody has to do it. We was going along picking up bodies off the doorsteps where their loved ones had dumped them. We came across this scruffy little feller in a doorway. The door was marked with a red cross or we wouldn't have taken him. Stuck him on the cart with the others and went off to the graveyard'.

with the others and went off to the graveyard'. His partner, Chris Cross (24-ish) added, 'We was just about to unload the cart when the bodies started moving, didn't they? Gave me a right turn, I can tell you. Turned out to be this singer trying to get out of the cart. What a mess. Bodies all over the place!'

SMELLY

Wandering minstrel Elwiss Prestley, of no fixed abode, said 'I'd had a few jars of ale and just sat down for a nap. Woke up under this fat, smelly feller. Thought it was somebody trying to muscle in on my sleeping spot. Told him to get off, didn't I? Course he didn't reply ... well, he wouldn't, him being dead like.'

TONIC

Sam and Chris were able to laugh about their grave mistake. 'We'll buy Elwiss a drink to make up for it,' Sam said. 'We can afford it – after all, business is good at the moment. They're dropping like flies.' Asked how he stays so fit and healthy Chris said he put it all down to 'Doctor Kurleus's Cureall Tonic'.

> ### Doctor Kurleus Cures All
> This is to give notice that John Kurleus, former physician to Charles I, offers a drink and pill that cures all sores, scabs, itch, scurfs, scurvies, leprosies and plagues be they ever so bad. There is no smoking or sweating or use of mercury or other dangerous and deadly substances. Doctor Kurleus sells the drink at three shillings to the quart and the pill one shilling a box. He lives at the Glass Lantern Tavern, Plough Yard in Grays Inn Lane
>
> He gives his opinion for nothing

THAT'S BETTER. NICE PURE AIR

bonfires were lit in the hope that they would 'purify' it.

No one understood that the real enemy was the rats, whose fleas spread the plague. That fact wasn't discovered until 1898.

Other doctors offered miracle cures for the plague. They would also offer free treatment, as in the advert (above). There was a catch, of course. Doctor Kurleus would look at a plague victim and say, 'You need a quart of my medicine. That'll be three shillings please.'

'I thought your advert said you give your opinion for nothing!'

'I do,' the devious doctor would shrug. 'My opinion is free, the drink is three shillings.'

Sick people, afraid of dying a painful plague death, would give anything for a cure. The fake doctors grew rich and the people died anyway.

Plague pottiness

Doctors said that dogs and cats, pigs, pet rabbits and pigeons could spread the plague. The government believed them and tried to prevent the plague by killing all the dogs in the town. Dogs were banned from towns and dog-killers were appointed to round up strays.

Other doctors blamed dirty air – huge

GUILTY!

WOEFUL WITCHES

BEING OLD WAS ALMOST A CRIME IN THE DAFT DAYS OF THE PAST. DO NOT GO BACK AS AN OLD WOMAN OR YOU MAY BE PUNISHED FOR BEING A 'WITCH' ... EVEN THOUGH THERE IS NO SUCH THING!

The witchfinder general

Britain's most famous witchfinder was Matthew Hopkins (died 1647) – the witchfinder general. Who gave him that name?

ACTUALLY I GAVE MYSELF THE NAME!

In the 1600s he was the terror of Suffolk, Essex and East Anglia, where he had around 230 people hanged as witches.

Here are six horrible Hopkins facts they never tell you...

1. The prisons became overcrowded with Hopkins victims. In summer the air was so filthy they died of disease. In fact, one report from Colchester in 1645 said...

The air was so foul that dogs, cats, mice and rats died and birds dropped from the sky.

As bad as the boys' toilets in one or two schools!

2. Hopkins thought there were a couple of ways to stop a witch's evil power. They were pretty disgusting so you might like to skip this bit.

HORRIBLE HISTORIES NOTE

Don't try this in the house as the smell will take days to clear.

YOU CAN BOIL A WITCH'S HAIR IN HER PEE... OR STICK A RED-HOT POKER IN HER POO. THAT WILL DESTROY HER MAGIC

3. Elizabeth Clarke of Chelmsford was sentenced to hang after Hopkins had accused her. She was taken to the gallows and told to climb the ladder.

But poor old Elizabeth only had one leg. She had to be helped up the ladder so a noose could be put around her neck. THEN the ladder was taken away and she was left to die.

4. Crowds rushed forward to grab a piece of a witch's clothes or the rope that hanged her. They wanted to snatch a bit of their magic.

So the hangmen took the bodies down as quickly as they could.

Sometimes they took them down TOO quickly. The victim was still alive.

They had to hang them again.

5. The witch was buried in a pit behind the jail. The corpse had a heavy rock placed on top. Sometimes they had a stake of wood driven through them.

This was to stop the witch rising up and going to heaven.

6. Hopkins made sure dozens of men and women hanged for witchcraft. That was the law in England. But ONE poor woman, Mary Lakeland, was burned alive.

Hopkins said she used her witchcraft to murder her husband. And the punishment for killing a husband was to burn. Mary Lakeland was perhaps the only witch to burn in England.

In 1645, in Ipswich she was…

❋ Dropped into a barrel of tar

❋ Chained to a post in the ground (so she couldn't jump out)

❋ Burned in the tar barrel with a bonfire underneath.

Witchfinder finish

There was a story that Matthew Hopkins was eventually tried as a witch and hanged. It would serve him right.

But that story is probably not true. He most likely died of a lung disease in 1647.

There were no more huge witch-hunts in England. The people found out it cost too much money to pay witchfinders, keep victims in prison and hang them. Hanging a witch cost £1 in the 1640s … a lot of money … while burning Mary Lakeland cost over £3.

Rowdy Revolutions

Kwick killer kwiz

1. A gunman called Zangara shot at US President Franklin D Roosevelt because he blamed the President for the pains in his stomach.

2. In 1981 US President Reagan was shot by John Hinckley because Hinckley wanted the actress Jodie Foster to take notice of him.

3. Queen Victoria was so popular no one ever tried to assassinate her though she reigned over 60 years.

4. US President Lincoln was shot dead even though he was guarded by 20 men.

5. In 1944 a bomb plot to kill Adolf Hitler only succeeded in blowing his trousers off.

6. Charles Guiteau shot President Garfield in 1881. After his execution his skull was put on display in the Washington Medical Museum where it can be seen today.

7. Indira Gandhi, Prime Minister of India, was shot by the men who were given the job of protecting her.

8. In 1835 a Corsican attacked King Louis Philippe of France and shot at him with 25 guns.

9. In 1835 a crazed gunman fired two pistols at US President Jackson and both pistols misfired. Yet the President had a bullet in his body.

10. As Caesar was stabbed to death in 44 BC he pulled his toga over his face so he couldn't see the knives.

WHAT'S SO FUNNY?

Answers:

1. True. Zangara went to a meeting, stood up on a chair to get a better view, took aim and fired.

2. True. President Reagan survived the stomach wound though his bodyguard was badly injured.

3. False. There were about eight attempts on Victoria's life.

4. False. President Lincoln was guarded by one policeman who sat outside the door to the President's gallery at the theatre.

5. True ... sort of. In July 1944 a bomb in a briefcase was placed under the table where Adolf Hitler was holding a meeting. By chance an officer moved the briefcase behind the leg of the heavy table. When it exploded it killed several people but the leg saved Hitler's life. He was deafened and suffered a numb arm and burns to his face ... but he lived. The greatest damage was to his trousers that were practically blown away and turned his famous moustache t' ash.

6. False. Guiteau did assassinate Garfield and his executed body was sent to surgeons to cut up for practice. The skull was put on display in Washington Medical Museum ... but it's not there now. Somebody pinched it and it has never been recovered!

7. True. Bodyguards make great assassins because they are in the best place to kill their victim. Mrs Gandhi's bodyguards were given the job of escorting her to a television interview, and they knew she wouldn't be wearing her bullet-proof vest in front of the cameras. After they filled her full of bullets they laid down their guns and raised their hands to surrender ... but no one came to arrest them. When the other guards heard the shooting they ran away and hid!

8. True. Guiseppe Fiesci rigged up a machine to fire 25 guns all at once. As King Louis Philippe went to inspect his troops Fiesci fired the world's first machine-gun and killed 18 people. But he missed his target, the King! Fiesci went to the guillotine; it didn't take 25 chops to kill him and the executioner didn't miss.

9. True. Jackson had gotten himself into a duel over a gambling debt. His rival's bullet hit close to his heart and stayed there. The second bullet was still there when the gunman shot at him in 1835.

10. False. Caesar let the top of his toga drop so it covered his legs. He didn't want to die with his legs showing. If the killers had had their way he'd have been showing more than his legs. They planned to strip him and throw his body in the river. But as he lay there dead they were horrified by what they'd done and they ran away. Three common slaves carried Caesar home instead.

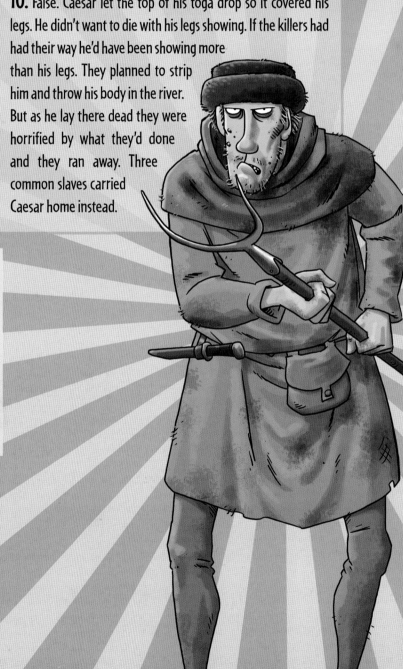

SUFFERING SLAVERY

WHAT IS THE HORRIBLEST THING TO BE IN HISTORY? IF YOU ASK ME IT'S BEING A SLAVE. SLAVES HAVE BEEN AROUND FOR THOUSANDS OF YEARS BUT IT BECAME BIG BUSINESS IN THE 1600S AND 1700S.

Slave suffering

In 1619, the first African slaves came to the English colonies in Virginia. Not all the slaves survived the horrible journey…

✸ These people were kidnapped from the west coast of Africa, tied to other captives by their hands and necks and marched along the coast to the African ports. Many died on this journey.

✸ They were packed on to ships with just half a metre for each captive. They were packed like books on a library shelf. Some were allowed exercise on deck – many weren't. Many died on this journey too.

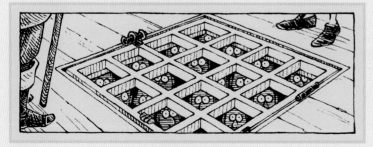

✸ If the suffocating air below decks didn't kill them then disease often did. Their only 'toilet' was an open bucket, shared by 100 people. A doctor looked in a diseased ship and reported…

The floor of their rooms was so covered with blood and mucus that it looked like a slaughterhouse.

✸ Dead slaves were simply thrown overboard. Those who lived were so weak that a quarter of them died in their first year in America.

WELCOME TO AMERICA, THE LAND OF THE FREE!

(America was called 'land of the free' in the song 'The Star Spangled Banner', written in 1814, 200 years after the first slaves landed in Virginia. Even in 1814 'land of the free' was still a joke! It became the USA National Anthem in 1931.)

From the 1660s states started to make laws to control their slaves. They said…

Guess what the punishment was for a white person who killed a slave?

That's right – the white person would not be punished unless it was deliberate murder … and then they got just three months in jail.

PLOTTING AGAINST WHITE OWNERS WILL BE PUNISHED BY DEATH.

Telling lies in court will be punished by…
1 Having an ear nailed to a post. 2 Being whipped. 3 Having the nailed ear cut off.
Meetings of four slaves or more are banned – even for funerals.
Striking a white person a second time will be punished by having the nose slit and the face burned.

Find that slave

Where did slaves come from? Mostly from Africa where African slave traders sold other Africans to the Brits. But where did they go to get a slave? After all, they couldn't just pop down to the local supermarket, pick up a few and flog them to the British slavers. Slave dealers in Africa either got them from tribes who had captured prisoners from other tribes in war or they simply kidnapped them.

Olaudah Equiano was captured when he was a child and sold as a slave. He is one of the few slaves who survived to write his own story. Olaudah said…

The grown-ups of our village used to go off to work in the fields. The children then gathered together to play. But whenever we played we always sent someone up a tree to watch out for the slave dealers. This was the time when slave dealers rushed into the village, snatched as many children as they could, and carried them off to the coast There they were sold as slaves.

Imagine that! You go to play in your local park and before you know it a gang has picked you up and sold you! You'd never see your home or your family again. Cruel.

Some slave dealers even got slaves from tribes who no longer wanted them in their tribe! A tribe might sell a criminal as a slave – which is a bit like your school selling you because you let down the head teacher's car tyres. (Actually, you probably deserve it!) But they also sold people who broke the rules of the tribe. One of the saddest cases was when they sold a woman whose 'crime' was … having twins!

GORGEOUS GEORGIANS

SOME OF THE MOST HORRIBLE THINGS IN HISTORY ARE THE THINGS PEOPLE DID TO THEMSELVES. WHAT THEY DID TO MAKE THEMSELVES LOOK BETTER.

Modern magazines offer readers a 'makeover' – they say they'll change someone's appearance from grot to hot in ten easy steps. If the Georgians did a makeover then the results would have been just as stunning …

1. White is beautiful, dear ladies,
Smear your face with paint of lead;
Never mind the lead has made
The men who mixed it ill … or dead.

~ Make-up is a flat white lead paint

YOU CAN DRAG A HORSE TO WATER BUT A FACE PAINT MUST BE LEAD

2. Take some silk of red or black,
Cut a circle or a crescent;
Stick it to your face to cover
Smallpox scars … it's much more pleasant.

~ Silk beauty spots are cut out and stuck on

DALMATIANS ARE VERY FASHIONABLE THIS YEAR

3. Take some plaster, dyed bright red,
Crush it to a ruby paste;
Smear it on your lips, dear ladies,
Never mind the chalky taste.

~ Red Plaster of Paris is used for lips

DON'T SMILE OR YOUR LIPS'LL DROP OFF

PLASTER

4. Shave your eyebrows clean away,
Take a trap and catch some mice;
Make false eyebrows from the mouse skin,
Stick them on to look so nice.

~ Black lead eyelashes and mouse-skin eyebrows are needed

CHEESE MADAM?

YUMMY!

YES PLEASE!

5. Make your face look sweet and chubby,
Pack your mouth with balls of cork;
Fit your false teeth in the middle,
Hope you don't choke when you talk.

~ Cork balls held in the cheeks improve the face

BUT MADAM, CRICKET BALLS ARE MADE OF CORK!

6. Next you need a monster wig
If you want to look real smashin';
When your wig has reached the ceiling
Then you'll be the height of fashion!

~ Build up the hair like a pyramid

I'M SURE MADAM'S UMBRELLA IS IN THERE SOMEWHERE

FOUL FRANCE

THE TROUBLE WITH BEING A KING OR QUEEN IS THAT PEOPLE BLAME YOU WHEN THINGS GO WRONG. BAD WEATHER MEANS BAD HARVEST MEANS HUNGRY PEOPLE. ARE YOU HUNGRY? BLAME THE KING. IN FRANCE IN 1793 THE STARVING PEASANTS DECIDED TO SLICE HIS HEAD OFF WITH A MACHINE CALLED THE 'GUILLOTINE'. WHERE WOULD YOU BUY A GUILLOTINE? IN THE CHOPPING CENTRE ... SHOPPING CENTRE, GEDDIT? OH, NEVER MIND.

The gruesome guillotine

The secret of speedy slicing was a machine that could kill kings cleanly and queens quickly, and lop lords and ladies like lightning. The guillotine.

Foul guillotine facts

1. The first French guillotine was built by Dr Joseph Guillotin ... but he had advice on how to build it. Who advised him? King Louis XVI. Imagine that. What must he have been thinking as he laid his head on the machine?

IT'LL BE INTERESTING TO SEE HOW OUR LITTLE INVENTION WORKS

WOW! THAT IS SERIOUSLY IMPRESSIVE!

2. Chopping French aristo heads started before the guillotines were built. The first day of the Revolution was 14 July 1789. On that day one nobleman, the Marquis of Launay, the governor of the Bastille, was caught by a Paris mob who cut off his head with a knife. His followers suffered the same charming chopping and their heads were paraded around Paris. The guillotine didn't replace the knife for another three years.

3. The guillotine is a famous machine of the French Revolution ... but head-chopping machines had been invented 200 years before. One was used in Halifax, northern England, to execute cattle thieves and one was used in Scotland when the Earl of Morton was executed on it in 1581. The Scots called it 'The Maiden'. Dr Guillotin pinched the English and Scottish idea.

4. The guillotine was quick, and good executioners could get through two victims a minute. Not easy.

5. The head shooting off from the guillotine became known as 'sneezing into the basket'. Atch-ouch. The guillotine itself was known as what?

a) The Red Theatre?
b) The People's Avenger?
c) The National Razor?

OH, WELL I NEEDED A SHAVE

Answer: All three.

6. The guillotine was tested first on live sheep and calves, then on dead bodies. Finally it was tried out on a live highwayman called Pelletier. Crowds turned out on 25 April 1792 to watch his execution. They went away grumbling, 'It was all over so quickly. It was no fun at all.' They marched off singing…

7. The French Revolution Terror from 1792 to 1794 sliced lots of heads off in two years – but the St Bartholomew's Day Massacre in 1572 killed more in one DAY.

8. One woman made a living by making wax masks from the dead heads in the guillotine basket. Her name was Madame Tussaud. Nice job.

9. Dr Guillotin invented the guillotine because he was such a kind man! He didn't want criminals to suffer. He said all they'd feel would be a tickle at the back of the neck. Oh yeah? Care to try it and prove it? One victim who felt nothing was called Valaze. He stabbed himself

to death in court in 1793 – but the judge said his corpse had to be guillotined anyway.

10. Some French doctors took a front seat at the executions to test if the head lived on after the chop. When the head fell they called out the victim's name. One reported…

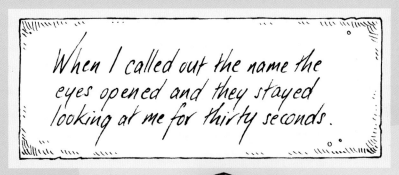

That's nonsense (you'll be pleased to know if you are ever sent to the guillotine).

Putrid Pirates

THE STORY 'PETER PAN' MAKES PIRATES LOOK FEARSOME AND WILD. THEY WEREN'T. THEY WERE JUST MUGGERS ON SHIPS. DESPERATE, CRUEL AND STUPID MEN. DO NOT CROSS CUTLASSES WITH A CORSAIR.

1. Pirates were often at sea for a long time so they took hens along (for eggs and meat). They also took 'hardtack' biscuits and limes. Their meat was often full of maggots and their biscuits were alive with weevils. They brushed some off and swallowed the rest.

2. On one island pirates were short of food so they had to eat snakes and monkeys.

3. When they needed to go to the loo they used a rope cage hanging over the sea.

4. When pirates buried treasure they would sometimes murder a prisoner and bury him on top of the treasure. That way the prisoner's ghost would guard the treasure. A sort of spook-curity guard. If they didn't have a prisoner then they might kill a member of the crew.

There was a sensible reason for this too. If the law came looking for the treasure they would say ...

A FRESH PILE OF EARTH, THEIR TREASURE IS THERE!

But when they dug down they would say…

NO, IT'S JUST A GRAVE. FILL IT IN AGAIN

5. Not many pirate ships had a doctor on board. So who cut off your leg or your arm if it was shattered in battle?

The carpenter, of course, because he was handy with the saw.

Or sometimes it would be the ship's cook who was good at carving up meat. That's neat.

Captain Ned Low enjoyed torturing his victims. But in one drunken attack he tangled with one of his own men and had his cheek slashed open.

The drunken ship's doctor tried to sew it up but Low didn't like it and told the doctor:

YOU COULDN'T SEW A BUTTON ON A SHIRT, YOU IDIOT!

FINE – SEE IF YOU CAN DO BETTER!

Low killed the doctor then did just what he said ... sewed up his own face. It left a scary scar. Just what a pirate wanted!

6. There were usually more rats on a ship than sailors.

Rats chewed the ropes, they chewed the wood and they even chewed the pirates. They also ate the food stored in the cabins.

Pirates would sometimes have rat hunts. One Spanish ship sailed from Europe to South America and had rat hunts along the way. The captain reported…

We killed 4,000 rats on that one journey

7. Pirates kept pets. They liked to take monkeys because they could sell them when they landed in Europe.

8. Pirates also kept working animals. Buccaneers kept dogs to help them with their hunting. Many ships carried cats. But the crew were very superstitious. Here is the rule…

1. If a black cat walks towards a sailor he will be lucky

2. If a black cat walks towards a sailor but then turns round and walks away he will be unlucky

3. If a black cat is thrown overboard a storm will follow and the ship will be cursed

9. The captain was in charge of the ship and you had to obey him in a battle. But when the crew were not fighting they could vote to have a new captain.

A 'good' pirate captain was one who helped his crew win lots of treasure.

A 'bad' pirate captain was usually a dead pirate captain.

OUR CAPTAIN IS HOPELESS

10. The worst job on a pirate ship was the job of 'powder monkey'. In a battle the powder monkey had to keep the gunners supplied with gunpowder. The job was usually given to boys about 11 or 12 years old – too young to fight with swords and pistols.

They were often kidnapped from their parents and forced to work. They were the youngest on the ship and the most bullied.

Powder monkey misery.

Useless USA

BRITISH EXPLORERS SET OFF ROUND THE WORLD TO EXPLORE STRANGE NEW WORLDS, TO SEEK OUT NEW LIFE AND NEW CIVILIZATIONS, TO BOLDLY GO WHERE NO MAN HAS GONE BEFORE ... AND THEN TO MURDER THE NATIVES, ROB THEIR LANDS OR DIE TRYING.

The vile Virginians

Many people think a group called the 'Pilgrim Fathers' were the first savage settlers from northern Europe. They weren't. There was a British colony set up ten years before in Virginia who went there to plunder the 'new' land. Here are some facts about them…

1. The Virginia invaders dug for gold in Jamestown instead of digging to plant crops. Of course they began to starve. In the winter of 1609 came the 'Starving Time'.

English settler, George Percy, wrote some disgusting descriptions of their sufferings…

> *We were driven, through hunger to eat things it is not natural to eat. We ate the flesh and the excrement of man. As well as our own people we ate an Indian after he had been buried for three days. We ate him all.*

Imagine eating 'excrement' … that's poo, if you didn't know!

DO YOU HAVE ANYTHING OTHER THAN ROTTING HUMAN FLESH?

POO PORRIDGE, POO PANCAKE, POO PATTIES, POO PASTY, POO PIZZA, POO PATE, POO PIE AND POO PUDDING

I'LL HAVE THE ROTTING HUMAN FLESH

2. After that some of the other tasty treats they ate must have seemed gorgeous! They ate dogs, rats, mice, snakes and horses.

WHAT'S THIS?

MICE CRISPIES!

CRUNCH CRUNCH

3. Don't tell your dad about this Virginian horror: a man killed his wife and began to eat her! He had begun to preserve her in salt (so she'd get him through the winter) when he was caught! The man was hanged … but not eaten.

HOW DO YOU FIND THE ACCUSED?

SALTY!

4. To add to their misery the Jamestown settlers fell ill. They suffered diseases like dysentery (where they had bloody poo) and one man died after…

> *His skin peeled off from head to foot*

The problem is that the water they were drinking was unhealthy stuff. George Percy said...

Our drink was cold water, taken from the river that was full of slime and filth.

It could be that they were drinking the water too close to the spot where their toilets drained into.

5. Life was tough for those early Virginia settlers – or 'Planters' as they called themselves. Between 1606 and 1625, 7,289 Planters landed and 6,040 of them were soon 'planted' in the ground, dead. Starvation, disease and Indian attacks killed them off.

6. In 2000 a scientist came up with a new idea. The Planters at Jamestown didn't die of hunger and disease. They died of poisoning!

The English and the Spanish hated one another and the Spanish didn't want the English in America. A war would have cost a lot of money. It was much easier to simply send a spy into the Jamestown settlement and poison the food or drink.

Arsenic would be the easiest poison to use. It has no taste or smell and there was a lot of it in Jamestown in the Planters' day. They used it to kill rats. Did someone use it to kill them?

SERVES THEM RIGHT

7. The Planters couldn't do much about the diseases, they could have been better farmers and they certainly could have made peace with the Indians ... but they weren't very good at it.

The Planters made a deal with the Indians on the Potomac river, a deal that meant 'friendship for life'. The Virginians kept to the deal easily ... because they made sure the 'life' of the Indians was very short.

'Join us in a drink!' the Virginians offered. The Indians drank the Planters' special ale ... but the Planters didn't drink it. The Indian chief, his family and 200 of his tribe dropped dead from poison. Vicious Virginians!

8. But the Indians could be guilty of cruelty and treachery too. Chief Opechancanough sent a peace party to talk to the Planters. They ate breakfast together, then the Indians grabbed whatever weapons they could find and slaughtered every man, woman and child they could catch! They killed 350 Planters when there were only about 1,000 in the whole of Virginia.

Twenty-two years later Chief Opechancanough said to the Planters, 'Why don't I send a peace party to talk with you?'

What would you have done if you'd been a settler? Said, 'No thanks, Ope, old chap!'?

The settlers said, 'Yes.'

What did Opechancanough's peace party do? They massacred over 300 of them again.

INDUSTRIAL REVOLUTION REGRETS

WHEN STEAM POWER CAME ALONG IN THE 1700S IT MEANT THERE WERE POWERFUL MACHINES THAT DID THE JOBS OF 20 WORKERS. WHAT HAPPENED TO THOSE 20 WORKERS? THEY LOST THEIR JOBS AND STARVED. AND STARVING PEOPLE REBEL AGAINST THE MACHINES. THEY DID IN SCOTLAND IN 1820 ... AND GAVE AN EXECUTIONER THE LAST EVER AXE-JOB IN BRITAIN.

The Flying Scot

CHOP! WEAVER WILSON PAYS PRICE

James Wilson, the 60-year old rebel leader, was brutally executed yesterday. The weavers' leader was fastened to a wooden sledge and dragged to a scaffold in front of the law courts in Glasgow. The old man wore an open-fronted shirt over his white prison uniform and white gloves. His mysterious travelling companion wore a black mask and carried an axe.

Last week Wilson was found guilty of treason. In April he had marched from the Lanarkshire village of Strathaven at the head of a small group of rebels. Wilson was armed with a rusty old sword and his followers had poor weapons. When they arrived in Glasgow they found the city was quiet and there was no support. They were easily arrested and brought to trial.

The judge sentenced him to suffer the ancient form of execution like William Wallace, to be hanged, drawn and quartered. A crowd of 20,000 gathered to watch the gruesome spectacle and there was a large guard of dragoon soldiers to prevent trouble.

Rebel head Wilson

Wilson was hanged and died bravely. He was then cut down and beheaded with a single stroke of the axe. The executioner held up the white-haired head and cried, 'Behold the head of a traitor,' as was the old custom. The crowd jeered and hissed in disgust, crying, 'Shame!' and 'Murder!'

Some of the soldiers fainted at the sight. It was decided to spare his corpse the disgrace of being cut into quarters. He was thrown into a pauper's grave in Glasgow but his niece had the body dug up and returned to the church-yard in his Strathaven home.

Wilson's supporters have been distributing handbills telling his true sad story and saying, 'May the ghost of the murdered Wilson haunt the pillow of his cruel judge.'

Next week the rebels Baird and Hardy will go to a similar death in Stirling. Isn't it time Scotland gave up this barbaric punishment? No man deserves to die the way Wilson died. The judge called him a 'miserable and sinful creature'. Many poor Scots will see him as a martyr for a free Scotland.

VILLAINOUS VICTORIANS

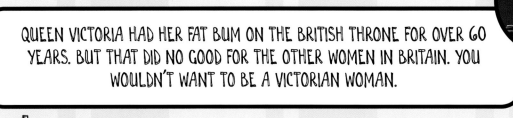

QUEEN VICTORIA HAD HER FAT BUM ON THE BRITISH THRONE FOR OVER 60 YEARS. BUT THAT DID NO GOOD FOR THE OTHER WOMEN IN BRITAIN. YOU WOULDN'T WANT TO BE A VICTORIAN WOMAN.

GOD SAVE OUR GRACIOUS ME

Women had a rotten time in Victoria's Britain. Husbands were allowed to beat their wives with sticks ... so long as the stick was no thicker than his thumb. And even if a young man was just a 'boyfriend' he treated a girl as if he owned her. One 16-year-old boy put it this way...

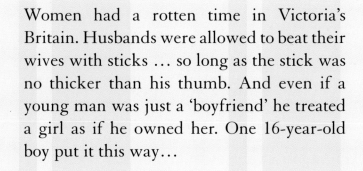

If I seed my gal talking to another chap I'd give her such a punch of the nose it would sharp put a stop to it.

HORRIBLE HISTORIES HINT TO BULLIES:
Notice he doesn't hit the 'chap'. Maybe because the 'chap' would hit him back? Remember – if you want to be a bully, be a coward first.

Some men even had the nerve to say...

It's an odd thing but the girls axully like a feller for walloping them. As long as the bruises hurt she'll be thinking of the bloke that gave them to her.

Sounds like a good excuse for the school bully, doesn't it? 'Actually, sir, the wimps love it when I hit them … so that's all right, isn't it?'

And if the boyfriends didn't beat the young women then their parents could do it instead. Some girls were sent out to sell things like apples. If they came back with the apples instead of the money, there was trouble…

Anyway, you can see why Victorian women grew up tough. And some grew up wicked. Take Elizabeth Pearson, for example…

Busy Lizzie

Elizabeth Pearson was 28 years old in 1875. She lived with her husband and son in Gainford, County Durham. Her uncle and aunt lived nearby and then her aunt died…

The jury did not say, 'Show her mercy'. So she was sent to hang at Durham Prison.

At 8 a.m. on the morning of 2 August 1875 Elizabeth Pearson was taken to the gallows with two other killers, both men. All three were to hang together. Elizabeth Pearson was the calmest of the three.

Her husband and son wept, but no one else did. At 8:03 a.m. a black flag was raised over the prison to show the executions had been completed. Villainous Victorian.

IREFUL IRISH

IN THE 1840S THE POOR PEASANTS OF IRELAND SURVIVED BY GROWING POTATOES. WHEN THOSE POTATOES BECAME DISEASED THEY STARVED HORRIBLY. DO NOT BE IRISH IN THE 1840S.

Foul famine

The good news for the poorest peasants in Ireland was that potatoes grew well in their fields. By the 1840s the most popular variety of spud was 'lumper' or 'horse potato'. It grew on the poorest land and gave a huge crop.

You just planted your potatoes in April and May, picked them in August, then they could be stored and eaten until following May. During summer your family had to buy oatmeal to eat until the next crop of spuds – this was the 'summer hunger' but it wasn't too bad. Some potatoes could be fed to your family pigs and they'd give you a bit of meat.

With the help of this super spud the population rose from 4.5 million in 1800 to 8 million in 1845. That was the good news. But the bad news was that you had no savings, because any spare money went to pay your landlord the rent. Still you survived … until 1845.

In August 1845 a fungus attacked the potatoes and it spread quickly over the country. The potatoes looked all right, but when you pulled them up they were black and rotten inside.

People went hungry and began to starve to death…

"Recently in Schull, County Cork, two small children wandered into the village crying that their dad wouldn't speak to them. Villagers took the children back to their home and found the father dead."

"I was sent to look at the grave of Kate Barry. I saw what looked like the tail of a horse lying there. I lifted it and pulled up her skull – the hair was Kate Barry's and her grave had been so shallow the dogs had dug her up and eaten her."

Asanath Nicholson – an American visitor said...

I was told of a cabin where in a dark corner lay a family of father, mother and two children lying together. The father was considerably rotted, whilst the mother had died last and had fastened the door so that their bodies would not be seen. Such family scenes were quite common. The cabin was simply pulled down over the corpses as a grave.

People would eat anything...

The countryside was emptied of its wildlife...

When the crop failed again in 1846 gangs of criminals formed known to the police as 'Ribbonmen'.

WE ATE THE BLOOD FROM A COW BAKED WITH VEGETABLES OR ANYTHING WE COULD FIND. DID YOU KNOW THAT YOU COULD TAKE TWO LITRES OF BLOOD FROM A LIVING COW BEFORE IT FALLS OVER?

SURE WE ATE THE DOGS FIRST, THEN THE DONKEYS, HORSES, FOXES, BADGERS, HEDGEHOGS AND EVEN FROGS. WE STEWED NETTLES AND DANDELIONS AND COLLECTED ALL THE NUTS AND BERRIES WE COULD FIND. THE PEOPLE ON THE COAST COULD EAT SHELLFISH BUT A LOT OF THEM WERE POISONOUS. MAYBE IT WAS BETTER A QUICK DEATH FROM POISONING THAN A SLOW ONE FROM HUNGER

MOST OF OUR CRIMES WERE STEALING FOOD AND MONEY. NOW THE PUNISHMENT FOR BEING CAUGHT WAS TO BE SENT TO AUSTRALIA... WHERE YOU'D BE WELL FED! SO IS IT ANY WONDER PEOPLE TURNED TO CRIME? ONE POOR WOMAN WAS CAUGHT STEALING FROM A FIELD. WHEN THE POLICE WHEN TO HER HOUSE THEY FOUND A POT BOILING WITH A FEW ROTTEN SPUDS AND A DOG IN IT

BARMY BRITISH EMPIRE

QUEEN VICTORIA DIDN'T JUST RULE BRITAIN SHE RULED AN EMPIRE OF ALL THE CONQUERED LANDS. YOU DON'T WANT TO BE A VICTIM OF THE BRITISH EMPIRE.

Terrifying Tasmania

The Aborigines of Tasmania had lived on their island, cut off from Australia, for 12,000 years. They were Stone Age people, but they got along well enough, and up to 20,000 lived on the island when the Brits arrived in 1802. Eighty years later there were NONE.

Where did these simple (and fairly harmless) people go? They were wiped out by a Great British idea.

WHAT A GREAT PLACE TO SEND OUR CONVICTS!

Of course there were convicts at Port Jackson in Australia. But how could you punish a really rotten convict who kept breaking the laws – a sort of 'super-convict'? Why not send him (or her) to Tasmania! No need to build a prison – just dump the convicts on the island and let them wander round to live or die…

…OR KILL

These wandering criminals were known as 'bushrangers' and they brought terror to the natives of Tasmania … the Aborigines. The bushrangers killed the Aborigines as if it were a game. Aborigine men were tied to trees and used for target practice. As one brutal bushranger said…

I'd shoot an Aborigine as easily as I'd shoot a sparrow. And at the same time I get a lot of fun from this sort of sport!

But they didn't stop there. A witness reported…

One bushranger, known as Carrots, killed an Aborigine man. Then he seized the dead man's wife. He cut off the man's head and fastened it round the wife's neck. Then he drove the weeping woman off to his den to be his slave.

Many Aborigine women were kept as slaves and chained in the bushranger homes till they were needed for work. One bushranger claimed…

Whenever I want her for anything I take a burning stick from the fire and press it on her skin!

The end

The Tasmanian Aborigines were vanishing.

❀ More Aborigines died of diseases the British brought and the tribes shrank.

❀ Settlers spread across the island and the British cattle replaced the Aborigines' kangaroos so the Aborigines starved. The tribes shrank again.

❀ The long-suffering natives finally stopped having children altogether and that eventually made the tribes die out entirely.

❀ Some Aborigines even began to slaughter their own children … babies can get in the way when you are fighting to survive.

In 1832 a 'kind' British Christian had 220 Aborigines shipped off to Flinders Island where they could make themselves a nice new home – except the Island was a bleak, cold place. The Aborigines could see their old home, Tasmania, across the water but they could never return. It's said that many died of home-sickness.

THEY CAN STOP ME LIVING THERE BUT THEY CAN'T STOP ME DYING HERE

In 1869 the last native Tasmanian man, King Billy, died of poisoning from drinking too much alcohol. But STILL the brutal Brits wouldn't let him rest. They wanted to study his body! So a surgeon…

❀ cut off his head.

❀ skinned the head and placed the skin on another skull.

❀ sent the head back to Britain.

Others cut off King Billy's hands and finally the whole body was stolen from the grave.

As you can imagine, the last woman, Truganini, was worried the same would happen to her corpse. She died in 1876, the last native Tasmanian. To save her being chopped and changed she was buried inside the walls of a prison. The plan didn't work though, and her bones ended up on display in Hobart Museum, Tasmania.

TRUGANINI THE LAST TASMANIAN

IT MUST BE NICE FOR HER TO BE HOME

Woeful First World War

IN 1914 BRITAIN AND HER FRIENDS WENT TO WAR WITH GERMANY AND HER FRIENDS. THIS WAS A WAR OF BOMBS AND MACHINE GUNS SO MILLIONS DIED. DO NOT BE A FIRST WORLD WAR SOLDIER WHO NEEDED THE TOILET.

There are no proper toilets in most of the Brit trenches, just buckets. If you upset the sergeant then you may be given the job of taking the buckets out after dark. Your job is to dig a hole and empty the buckets.

Perilous Pee

Once you are out of the cover of the trenches you are in danger, of course. But some soldiers still light cigarettes to hide the smell from the buckets. Enemy snipers are just waiting to aim at the glow of a cigarette end.

EMPTYING TOILET BUCKETS CAN BE BAD FOR YOUR HEALTH

Even going to the toilet shed just behind the trenches can be dangerous. The enemy know men use these toilets at dawn and like to drop a few shells among the toilet huts to catch the soldiers with their pants down!

HAVING A POO CAN BE BAD FOR YOUR HEALTH

Bucket and chuck it

In the 1917 battles in Flanders the troops do not have proper trenches, just shell holes and sandbags. There are no toilet huts. One officer writes home…

If you want to do your daily job of urinating and otherwise there is an empty tin can, and you have to do that in front of all your men, and then chuck the contents (but not the tin can) out over the back.

ENEMY

GENERALS

He forgot to say one important thing. Find out which way the wind is blowing first!

And being a German soldier was just as bad. Soldiers need toilets the same as the people back home. The trouble is they don't have nice comfy ones like you!

Terrible toilets

What does a German soldier do when he is not in the trenches – the 'front line'? What would you do to relax? Sleep? Write letters to your family? Clean your toenails? No. You'd go to the toilet for a chat.

Erich Maria Remarque is the author of the famous War book, All Quiet on the Western Front. He says…

The older soldiers don't use the unpleasant, indoor, common toilet, where 20 men sit side-by-side in a line. As it is not raining, they use the individual square wooden boxes with carrying handles on the sides. They pull three into a circle and sit there in the sun all afternoon, reading, smoking, talking, playing cards.

ONE DAY IN THE TRENCHES...

HI CARL! BUSY?

ME? NO, NOT REALLY

FANCY A POO?

OOOH LOVELY

NOSES ARE RED, MY FEET ARE BLUE, THERE'S LICE IN MY PANTS, AND THE RATS ATE THE STEW

Toilets are built just behind the trenches out of sight of the enemy. They are usually deep pits with wooden seats on top. When the pit is full it is closed and another one dug.

TERRIBLE TWENTIES

EVERY TIME IN HISTORY HAS ITS HORRIBLE BITS. IN THE 1920S AMERICA TRIED TO BAN BOOZE. GANGS STARTED TO MAKE ALCOHOL AND SELL IT AND MAKE A LOT OF MONEY. THEN THEY SQUABBLED WITH RIVAL GANGS. NEVER BE A GANGSTER ... YOU MAY FACE EXECUTIONERS CRUELLER THAN ME.

Happy Valentine's Day, you guys!

Prohibition meant big money for the men who sold the illegal booze. But they had to protect the money with some pretty violent men. One of the most vicious gang leaders was Big Al Capone who sold booze in Chicago. And it didn't pay to upset Big Al.

One man who tried to steal Capone's business was 'Bugs' Moran. Al Capone set up a very special Valentine's Day gift for 'Bugs', then Al went on holiday to Florida. The amazing thing about the story was the way it appeared in the newspapers the next day!

The Chicago Herald

15 FEB 1929

COPS CHOP BUGS BOYS

Last night seven members of the Bugs Moran gang died in a hail of machine-gun bullets.

On St Valentine's Day, last night, the men arrived at a warehouse in Clarke Street to wait for a truckload of stolen whiskey. But there was no whiskey — only death in a police trap.

A local resident, Andy Reiss, described the scene: 'I heard a truck door slam and looked out of my window opposite the warehouse. I saw two cops in uniform and two plain-clothes detectives get out of a police wagon. They ran into the warehouse. That's when I heard a sound like a pneumatic drill — I guess that was the machine- gun! Then the two uniformed cops came out with their guns pointed at two other men. It all went quiet for a while then we heard the guard dog begin to howl. It didn't stop so we went across to investigate.'

Reiss's neighbour (who did not wish to give his name) said, 'The door was open so we went in. It was like a slaughterhouse in there. There were seven bodies. The cops had just lined them up against the wall and blasted them. The blood was flooding over the floor and into the drain. The only sound was one guy moaning. We went and called for an ambulance but it was too late for him. It's a bit of a shock to think the police can murder men in cold blood like that!'

The neighbour's wife added, 'Moran's gang stole booze from a police gang two weeks ago. Bet ya this was their revenge!'

The police chief denies that the Chicago police force had anything to do with the massacre.

Our reporter tracked down 'Bugs' Moran to his home today. Moran agreed the men were members of his gang but insisted, 'That was meant to be me in there! I stopped off for a cup of coffee so I was late. I saw the police run in and I escaped with my life. But I thought it was just an ordinary raid! I just can't believe the police would do this to my boys. We pay the cops too well. Only Capone kills like that!' The investigation continues.

AL CAPONE — INVOLVED?

The newspapers got some of the facts right but one important one wrong … the killers were NOT the Chicago police. They were Al Capone's gang dressed up as police. They fooled their victims, who lined up against the wall to be searched, and they fooled the witnesses.

The four killers were never punished for the St Valentine's Day massacre, but two died horribly anyway. These two, Anesimi and Scalise, agreed to turn on their boss, Al Capone, and kill him. Big Al heard about their plot and planned a suitable revenge. Capone arranged a big dinner party where Anesimi and Scalise were the main guests. Al gave a speech and talked about how important it was to be loyal to your boss. Then he had Anesimi and Scalise tied to their chairs. He took out a baseball bat and, in front of his guests, battered the heads of the traitors till they were dead.

If that's not enough to put you off your dinner, what is?

SPIES OF WORLD WAR 2

YOU'VE SEEN JAMES BOND MOVIES. SPIES ARE CLEVER MEN WHO NEVER GET KILLED? FORGET THAT. IN WORLD WAR 2 MANY WOMEN WERE SPIES ... AND SOME DIED HORRIBLY. DO NOT BE A WORLD WAR 2 SPY OR YOU MAY END UP MEETING ONE OF MY EXECUTIONER PALS.

Louise (Violette Szabo) 1921–1945

Violette was just 20 when she met a French soldier, Etienne Szabo, and married him in London.

Etienne went off to fight against Germany and was killed. Violette wanted revenge. She left her baby daughter and trained to fight with the Resistance in France.

Her first job was dangerous…

GO TO FRANCE AND JOIN THE RESISTANCE AT ROUEN. A LOT OF THEM HAVE BEEN CAPTURED. WE WANT TO FIND OUT WHY

Violette did a great job even though she was arrested twice. She flew back to London.

Her second trip didn't have such a happy ending.

On 10 June 1944 she was with the Resistance leader when they ran into a troop of German soldiers…

VIOLETTE AND THE FRENCHMAN RAN…

HALT!

WE CAN MAKE IT!

BUT VIOLETTE FELL AND TWISTED HER ANKLE…

SAVE YOURSELF, PLEASE. I'LL COVER YOU!

VIOLETTE FIRED TILL SHE RAN OUT OF BULLETS. THEN SHE WAS CAPTURED…

WHERE IS YOUR FRIEND?

I'M ALONE!

SHE WAS TAKEN AND TORTURED…

NOOOOOOOO!

VIOLETTE WAS TAKEN TO RAVENSBRÜCK CAMP AND SET TO DO HARD LABOUR. IN FEBRUARY, SHE WAS EXECUTED

Nancy Wake (1912–2011)

Nancy Wake was an Australian who helped the French Resistance in Marseilles at the start of the war. She escaped to England, but had to leave her husband behind. Nancy trained with the SOE and returned to France to help the Resistance at Auvergne.

Nancy got a shock when the Resistance leader Gaspart said…

WE WILL TAKE YOUR WEAPONS BUT WE WON'T TAKE ORDERS FROM YOU BRITISH!

AUSTRALIAN, ACTUALLY

When Nancy argued they said they'd shoot her. Just in time a radio operator, Denis Rake, landed and showed how useful the SOE could be.

Nancy sent radio messages for more weapons. She cycled from Resistance group to Resistance group, taking orders and having guns dropped.

A massive German force of 22,000 troops was sent to crush them. Nancy drove across the battlefield, delivering bullets and carrying the wounded to safety.

In the gun battle Denis Rake's radio was wrecked. Nancy set off on her bike to find the nearest SOE radio. There was not enough petrol for such a long journey and the tracks were too narrow and rocky to go by car.

TIME TO GET ON YER BIKE!

She cycled for 36 hours to send a signal to Britain. Then she cycled straight back to the battlefield – another 36 hours. She was tired and bleeding, but she saved the Resistance. They won the battle.

After the war she went back to Marseilles to find her husband. She was told…

YOUR HUSBAND WAS CAPTURED SOON AFTER YOU LEFT. THEY TORTURED HIM THEN SHOT HIM

Odette Sansom (1912–1995)

Odette landed near Cassis in November 1942. She worked with SOE fighters and became a messenger to one of them, Peter Churchill (1909–1972). They were arrested by a German who had pretended to be a friend. Odette was tortured and tried to say Peter Churchill was innocent. Finally she told the Germans that (a) Peter was her husband and (b) Brit Prime Minister Winston Churchill was his uncle. The Germans believed her and set her free.

Blitzed Brits

IMAGINE YOU ARE TOLD TO LEAVE YOUR HOME AND TO GO AND LIVE WITH STRANGERS. HOW HORRIBLE IS THAT? IT'S WHAT HAPPENED TO MILLIONS OF CHILDREN IN WORLD WAR 2.

World War Three! – Hosts v Evacuees

Which was worse … being an evacuee, or being a host in the country who had the job of living with the evacuees? There are two sides to every argument.

This is what the hosts said...

Host: You couldn't buy a small-tooth comb anywhere in Northallerton. They'd all been bought because a lot of the evacuees came with fleas in their hair.

Host's daughter: I came home from work one day and found two youths, nearly as tall as my father. They'd told mother we had to take them because we had a spare bedroom.

Host's daughter: There were five of us in a three-bedroom house. When we took an evacuee it meant my brother had to share my bedroom. I resented this, as I took an instant dislike to the lad who came to stay with us.

Host's daughter: Our evacuees arrived in shabby clothes so mother gave them new ones. They were allowed home on a visit and came back with more old clothes. Their parents had sold the new ones we'd given them!

Host's daughter: Our new evacuee was a terror. One day he was playing with matches and he set fire to a chair. We had to decorate after he left. The door was covered with dart holes and the walls with writing.

Hostess: My father used to say he never saw anything like our evacuees – they never shed a tear when their parents left for home.

Hostess: We had three brothers aged four to eight. They had no idea of food other than chips. They didn't know how to eat a boiled egg.

BUT some said...

Host's daughter: My parents took a boy of six. He was really a wonderful child in every way. He was brought up by my parents as one of the family. His mother came and stayed long weekends and holidays with us.

On the other hand, this is what the evacuees said...

Girl evacuee aged seven: The farm was three miles from the village and had only cold water which had to be pumped up into the kitchen.

Girl evacuee aged seven: The toilet was at the end of a long garden and was just a pit in the ground filled with ashes. It had two holes. The farmer's daughter and I always went together, particularly in the dark.

Girl evacuee: I remember my eleventh birthday. Mrs Spencer took me seven miles to see Tarzan of the Apes. But there was only a bus there. We had to walk back.

Girl evacuee aged nine: We fed the chickens each day. I thought they were pets and was heartbroken when I saw the first one killed and plucked. I once witnessed the slaughter of a pig. It was so distressing that I started having nightmares. I was firmly told that this was their way of life. I was a very silly, spoilt child who knew nothing.

Girl evacuee aged seven: One thing that upset me was that the only farm worker was not allowed to sit at the table with the family. He had to have his meal at a separate table.

Boy evacuee aged twelve: There were lots of apple and pear orchards. We thought you could just help yourself. The village kids told us we shouldn't do it. The police came to see our hosts and they put a stop to it.

Girl evacuee aged nine: Anything wrong in the house was always my fault because the farmer's daughters ganged together. They broke my only doll and tore my books. When mum collected me she was in tears. She could see every bone in my body.

BUT some had happy memories...

Girl evacuee aged eight: We helped on the farm at weekends. I used to like watching the milking done. It was done by hand. We used to love the lambing season when we could go and see the lambs after they were born. It was all new to us. In the town we only had factories and shipyards.

EPILOGUE

YOU SEE? HISTORY WAS HORRIBLE. AND THE BAD NEWS IS THE WORLD CAN STILL BE A NASTY PLACE FROM TIME TO TIME.
EXECUTIONERS? WE'VE BEEN AROUND A FEW THOUSAND YEARS. EXECUTING PEOPLE. SOME OF MY VICTIMS WERE WICKED. SOME WERE SAINTS. MY FRIENDS DON'T GET TO USE THE OLD AXE SO MUCH THESE DAYS. MY EXECUTIONER FRIENDS DON'T NEED TO. THEY HAVE BULLETS AND BOMBS AND POISONS AND PLASTIC EXPLOSIVES.
THE PAST IS JUST ONE LONG, HORRIBLE, GORY STORY.

Oh, all right. History could be horrible some of the time. But most of the time it was :

DIRTY

Even Queens like Elizabeth I said…

I take a bath four times a year … whether I need one or not.

CRUEL

The Romans went to watch people die painfully in the arenas the way we go to watch football…

DANGEROUS

You could be killed by a flea, and millions were. (Not the same flea, obviously). Fleas carried the Black Death and nobody knew the little hoppers were to blame. After all everyone had ordinary fleas and plague fleas look almost the same …

The food was foul and the toilets were terrible. The only GOOD thing about the olden days was most people didn't have to go to school.

So history was mostly disgusting but boring. Still, from time to time something truly horrible happened. The Horrible Histories books have been collecting these twisted tales for twenty years. And here are the most horrible of the horrible and a lesson to us all. Just don't ask me what that lesson is … something about having a bath once a month, and don't get into a fight with a man eating lion … or a flea.